Intrepid Laughter

PRESTON STURGES AND THE MOVIES

by ANDREW DICKOS

UNIVERSITY PRESS OF KENTUCKY

Scholarly publisher for the Commonwealth,
serving Bellarmine University, Berea College, Centre
College of Kentucky, Eastern Kentucky University,
The Filson Historical Society, Georgetown College,
Kentucky Historical Society, Kentucky State University,
Morehead State University, Murray State University,
Northern Kentucky University, Transylvania University,
University of Kentucky, University of Louisville,
and Western Kentucky University.
All rights reserved.

Editorial and Sales Offices: The University Press of Kentucky
663 South Limestone Street, Lexington, Kentucky 40508-4008
www.kentuckypress.com

17 16 15 14 13   5 4 3 2 1

Frontispiece photo of Preston Sturges (1941),
courtesy The Museum of Modern Art/Film Stills Archive

The photos on pages 6, 8, and 12 are reproduced by permission of the
Performing Arts Research Center, The New York Public Library at Lincoln
Center; Astor, Lennox, and Tilden Foundations.

The Library of Congress has cataloged the Scarecrow Press edition
of this book as follows:

Dickos, Andrew, 1952–
   Intrepid laughter.

   Bibliography: p.
   Filmography: p.
   Includes index.
   1. Sturges, Preston. I. Title
PN1998.A3S886 1985   812'.52   85-2512

ISBN 978-0-8131-4194-7 (pbk.: alk. paper)

This book is printed on acid-free paper meeting
the requirements of the American National Standard
for Permanence in Paper for Printed Library Materials.

Manufactured in the United States of America.

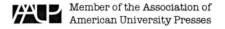 Member of the Association of
American University Presses

Screen Classics

Screen Classics is a series of critical biographies, film histories, and analytical studies focusing on neglected filmmakers and important screen artists and subjects, from the era of silent cinema to the golden age of Hollywood to the international generation of today. Books in the Screen Classics series are intended for scholars and general readers alike. The contributing authors are established figures in their respective fields. This series also serves the purpose of advancing scholarship on film personalities and themes with ties to Kentucky.

Series Editor
Patrick McGilligan

Books in the Series

Mae Murray: The Girl with the Bee-Stung Lips
Michael G. Ankerich

Hedy Lamarr: The Most Beautiful Woman in Film
Ruth Barton

Von Sternberg
John Baxter

The Marxist and the Movies: A Biography of Paul Jarrico
Larry Ceplair

Warren Oates: A Wild Life
Susan Compo

Jack Nicholson: The Early Years
Robert Crane and Christopher Fryer

Being Hal Ashby: Life of a Hollywood Rebel
Nick Dawson

Intrepid Laughter: Preston Sturges and the Movies
Andrew Dickos

John Gilbert: The Last of the Silent Film Stars
Eve Golden

For my mother
and in memory of
Charlotte Seideman Whisenhunt

CONTENTS

PREFACE

When a Hollywood phenomenon like Preston Sturges occurs, the desire to analyze it, to uncover the intrinsic meaning lying at its core, may kill the brilliance that makes it unique. The fact is, Preston Sturges is so much more than the sum of his parts--screenwriter, slapstick artist, cynic, wit, satirist, sentimentalist--that explicating his style offers insight into his sensibility, but cannot deliver that total, full-bodied, savor of Sturges' universe that watching his films does. I think the sensitive viewer realizes this dilemma and understands that it arises less from a critical inability to discuss his work than from an awareness that Sturges' films contain a magic that originates in the peculiar experience of watching a movie. This is hardly an attempt to undermine the art of criticism, but simply a realization that a vital difference exists between watching a Sturges movie and writing about it.

Other screenwriters have inherited the director's chair in the course of their careers, but none has conquered it the way Preston Sturges did. John Huston and Billy Wilder revealed a fusion of their visual and literary styles; however, more intermittently than consistently in view of their total outputs. But with a filmography consisting of a dozen works, half of which are among the most memorable comedies in the history of American sound film, Sturges proved without question that the writer-auteur can become a greater auteur when placed behind the camera. In Sturges' case, it relied less on the ability to parallel the script with a visual style than a thrustful effort to meld camera movement, kinetic compositions, sharply defined character parts, witty dialogue, and carefully crafted plots. The synthesis of every aspect of narrative cinema propels his films, and ultimately they are special because we appreciate each element operating separately in full gear yet in unison with the others.

Sturges perfected this synthesis in The Miracle of Morgan's Creek; but even in his first film, The Great McGinty, the engagement between the formal and thematic elements of his style clearly establishes his alternative vision of America as a land where, as Andrew Sarris notes, "the lowliest boob could rise to the top with the right degree of luck, bluff, and fraud."[1] And from <u>McGinty</u> on, the sheer frantic energy expended in Sturges' world illustrates our American spirit--our need always to be moving somewhere--and his characters, pushing and shoving their way across the screen, become part of the uncontrollable momentum gathered by this spirit. In fact, Sturges' characters emerge as still greater functions in this setting: they become demons of invigorating originality and self-aggrandizement, of the hope that with self-assertion will come at least a brief moment of screen immortality.

The biographical sketch of Preston Sturges aims to inform the reader of a remarkably rich life. This brief account is not intended as a background for psychological speculation; it was written to show the vast number of influences--people, places, and events--that shaped Sturges' life and affected his creative activity. It has been said that a chronicle of Preston Sturges' life would have made an incredible and highly unsalable scenario, so improbable and ironic are many moments of it. It is, therefore, as an illustration of this unique life lived and the references, attitudes, and motifs extracted from it and apparent in Sturges' screen work that this section is included.

In the screenwriting section, I discuss the structure and style of Sturges' screenwriting, particularly of his comedies, and draw some connections to the dramatic heritage behind them. Most all of the screenplay references are from the latest typescript versions in the Department of Special Collections or the Theatre Arts Library of the University Research Library at the University of California, Los Angeles.

And the section on the twelve films written and directed by Sturges is my commentary, useful, I hope, as much for what it contains as for the omissions that any caring reader would be provoked to find.

A. D.
New York
1983

ACKNOWLEDGMENTS

My gratitude goes to Professor William Everson of the Cinema Studies Department, New York University, whose unstinting generosity in this project cannot be overestimated. I am also grateful to Brooke Whiting of the Department of Special Collections, University Research Library, U. C. L. A. , and Anita Lowry of the Reference Department, Columbia University Library, for their assistance.

Special thanks go to Marva Nabili, Thomas Fucci, Grafton Nunes, Ilene Singh, James T. Kelly, and Anastasia and Peter Panos for their various--and in many cases, most generous--help.

Acknowledgment is also made to Paula Klaw of Movie Star News and to Mary Corliss of the Museum of Modern Art/ Film Stills Archive.

Finally, I am indebted to Sandy Sturges for correcting the manuscript of the biographical profile, for permission to use her late husband's private papers, and for the hours of memorable and indispensable conversation provided in friendship. Her encouragement and openness made the completion of this book a special pleasure.

CHRONOLOGY

1898-   August 29th. Preston Sturges born in Chicago, Il-
         linois to Mary Estelle Dempsey and Edmund Biden.

1901-   January? Leaves America for the first time with
         his mother to spend most of his childhood in Eu-
         rope. Visits intermittently in America during his
         childhood years.

1902-   January. Adopted by Solomon Sturges.

1907-14- Attends schools in France and Switzerland.

1911-   Mary Sturges (Desti) opens Maison Desti in Paris.

1914-   Summer. Manages the Deauville branch of Maison
         Desti.
         Autumn. Returns to America; sees his father,
         Solomon, for the first time since early childhood.

1915-17- Runs the Desti emporium in New York.

1916-   Works as a runner for stockbrokers F.B. Keech in
         New York.

1917-   July. Enlists in the air service. Sent to Camp
         Dick in Texas where he graduates as lieutenant in
         the Sixty-Third Squadron. Publishes his first piece
         of writing, "300 Words of Humor," in the camp
         newspaper.

1919-27- Returns to New York to Keech, then to resume
         management of the Desti emporium and to work on
         his inventions.

1920-   Closes the retail operation of Desti cosmetics.

1923-   December. Marries Estelle de Wolfe Mudge of
         Bristol, Rhode Island.

1927-   Estelle Mudge and Sturges divorce.
         Christmas.   Stricken with appendicitis in Chicago.
         Writes Speaking of Operations during his recupera-
         tion.

1928-   First completed full-length play, The Guinea Pig,
         staged at the Wharf Players Theatre in Province-
         town on July 30th.   Later, it goes to Broadway.

1929-   Strictly Dishonorable produced on Broadway by
         Brock Pemberton and directed by Antoinette Perry.
         The Big Pond, Sturges' first screenplay, written
         for Paramount.

1930-   January.   Stages his next play, Recapture.
         The Well of Romance, an operetta written with
         Maurice Jacquet, staged.
         April.   Marries Eleanor Post Hutton.
         Writes the dialogue for Paramount's Fast and
         Loose.

1931-   April.   Mary Desti dies.

1932-   March.   Child of Manhattan staged.
         April.   Eleanor Hutton and Sturges divorce.
         September.   Moves to Hollywood to write the
         screenplay for Universal's The Invisible Man.
         Late.   Writes The Power and the Glory for Fox.

1934-   Writes Thirty-Day Princess for Paramount.
         Late.   Writes The Good Fairy for Paramount.

1935-   Writes Diamond Jim for Paramount.

1936-   Writes Hotel Haywire for Paramount.

1937-   Writes Easy Living for Paramount.
         Opens the Sturges Engineering Company.
         Late.   Writes Port of Seven Seas with Ernest
         Vajda for M-G-M.

1938-   Writes If I Were King for Paramount.
         Late.   Works on the script of Never Say Die for
         Paramount.
         November.   Marries Louise Sargent Tevis.

1939-   Writes Remember the Night for Paramount.

1940-   May. Solomon Sturges dies.
          July. Opens The Players Restaurant and Drive-In.
          July. Sturges' first directed film, The Great Mc-
          Ginty, released by Paramount.
          September. Christmas in July released by Para-
          mount.

1941-   February. The Lady Eve released by Paramount.
          June. Solomon (Mon) Sturges IV born.
          The Players reopens as The Players Club.
          December. Sullivan's Travels released by Para-
          mount.

1942-   Early. Produces and writes some of René Clair's
          I Married a Witch for Paramount.
          Writes Triumph over Pain (The Great Moment) and
          begins work on The Miracle of Morgan's Creek.
          November. The Palm Beach Story released by
          Paramount.

1943-   Works on The Miracle of Morgan's Creek.

1944-   January. The Miracle of Morgan's Creek released
          by Paramount.
          January. Leaves Paramount.
          February. Forms California Pictures Corporation
          with Howard Hughes.
          June. Hail the Conquering Hero and The Great
          Moment released by Paramount.

1945-   Works on subsequently aborted production of Ven-
          detta.
          September. Starts shooting The Sin of Harold Did-
          dlebock.

1946-   May. Louise Tevis and Sturges divorce.
          October. Resigns as an officer of California Pic-
          tures.
          December. Signs a contract with Twentieth Century-
          Fox.

1947-   April. The Sin of Harold Diddlebock released by
          United Artists.

1948-   October. Unfaithfully Yours released by Fox.

1949-   May. The Beautiful Blonde from Bashful Bend

released by Fox.
Leaves Fox.
Late. Works on various screenplays.

1950-51- Writes the book for the musical Make a Wish, based on his own screenplay of The Good Fairy.

1950- The Sin of Harold Diddlebock rereleased as Mad Wednesday after reediting by Howard Hughes.

1951-59- Works on various unproduced stage and screen projects.

1951- April. Completes conversion of The Players into a dinner theatre.
August. Marries Anne "Sandy" Nagle.

1953- February. Preston Sturges, Jr. born.
The Players and the Sturges Engineering Company close.

1954- January. Leaves for Europe.

1954-55- Works on his last film, The Notebooks of Major Thompson (The French They Are a Funny Race) in Paris.

1956- June. Thomas Preston Sturges born.

1957- May. The French They Are a Funny Race released in America by Continental Distributors.

1959- Early. Works on autobiography for Henry Holt.
August 6th. Preston Sturges dies in New York.

THE MOST BIZARRE AND MARVELOUS SCENARIO:
FLASHBACKS ON THE LIFE AND
CAREER OF PRESTON STURGES

A kaleidoscopic whirl of extraordinary people and improbable events clearly does not represent most lives. Of the few people with the vision and energy to command greatness, most end up accepting less, settling for life as a project of trying to find pleasure, resignedly, in the ordinary. They have not found themselves in the right place at the right time or expended their imaginative energy to realize the concrete act. Or, they simply have not been blessed. Preston Sturges lived a life that could fuel a score of pictures with wonderful story lines and complications to rival even his own masterpieces. Such lives are adjuncts to other artists' careers, as well, and certainly not a critical factor in the judgment of their work. Here, Sturges' films do indeed stand alone, just as his life stands apart from other lives as of a piece, as of a work by a biographee in search of an extended tale. But the connecting thread between Sturges' life and his art is peculiar with him: perhaps because the attempt to see reference points and moments in his work is an eerie investigation into the connection between life and the cinema, between the powerful imagination behind such a marvelous life and the power of an illusionist medium to represent this artist's imagination.

Any account of Sturges' early life cannot ignore the dominant presence of his mother, Mary Desti, and many of her adventures are mirrored through Preston Sturges' eyes, both as a young observer and sometime participant and, much later, as an autobiographer. She was not exactly a smothering woman as much as a free-spirited and often impetuous presence with boundless and passionate flair. Mary did not defy the conventions of her day; she simply walked away from them, unaware of making any repudiating gesture. So, at the turn of the century, she left her husband of the moment to embark on a singing career in Paris with little Preston in tow. Mary literally exposed him to the experiences of a lifetime.

Her soon-to-be lifelong friend, Isadora Duncan, and her brothers; Paris Singer; Aleister Crowley; exotic Turks; prewar Paris; and summers across the face of Europe became the characters and locales of Sturges' childhood. This was Europe. Sturges lived his youth here in America: in New York; in Chicago with his much-admired adoptive father, Solomon; in pursuit of his inventions; and in endeavoring to market Mary Desti's famous cosmetics. All this preceded his decision at twenty-nine to write his first play, followed by a writing career that would bring him Broadway success and ultimately lead him to Hollywood and an unparalleled movie-making adventure. To ignore such wonderful diversions in a study of Sturges' work would sadly deprive the reader of a glimpse of a rich and panoramic life, complete, as it were, with the stuff of movies.

The Cultural Manifesto of an Eccentric Crossbreeding: Sturges as a Kid

> I don't believe environment has the slightest bit to
> do with anything--I only believe in ancestral influ-
> ence. It would have made no difference whether I'd
> been brought up in a reform school, or on the Island
> of Lesbos.
> --Preston Sturges (1945)[1]

"No such plebian name as Dempsey could possibly have been hers," Sturges wrote.

> With this as a starter it was but one leap to the
> conclusion that the name was a misnomer, bestowed
> upon us in error by the vulgar Irish varlets of her
> ancestor, a distinguished Italian prince, unfortunate-
> ly on the lam in Ireland because of a romantic duel.
> What these flunkies were trying to say was 'd'Este,'
> the gentleman being a member of that celebrated
> Italian family ... only they couldn't pronounce it.
> Thus my mother, actually an Italian princess, re-
> sumed her true name and became Mary d'Este Demp-
> sey, a monicker that adorns most of her works and
> many of her marriage certificates. [2]

"My mother was in no sense a liar, nor even mildly unacquainted with the truth ... as she knew it," Sturges cautioned. "She was endowed with such a rich and powerful

imagination that anything she had said three times she be-
lieved fervently. Often twice was enough. "[3]

Preston's natural father, Edmund Biden, was a travel-
ing salesman and Mary's second husband. Disillusioned and
exhausted by his bouts of drunken rage and unpredictable behavior, she had their marriage annulled. "Mr. Biden never
sounded like much of a husband to me," Sturges recalled,
"but it must be remembered that he was one of Mother's first
ones and that she did better later. "[4]

On the advice of Dr. Ziegfeld, Florenz Ziegfeld's
father and then head of the Chicago Musical College, Mary
sailed for Paris to pursue a singing career. "At this moment I had rather an extraordinary voice," she wrote, "and,
as I was scarcely more than a child myself, great things were
hoped for from my Paris trip. "[5] She was twenty-nine at the
time; but "if it pleased her to be 'scarcely more than a child
myself' in Paris in 1901," remarked Sturges later in his life,
"that is perfectly all right with me. I am probably lucky
that she never introduced me as her brother. "[6] Mary arrived in Paris with very little money and no place to go.
That night she bathed baby Preston in a cold water bath down
the corridor of a rather unfortunate inn at 5 Avenue d'Antin
where they managed to get a room.

It was at this time that Mary was introduced to Isadora
Duncan, her brother Raymond, and their mother, new arri-
vals in Paris themselves, in the real estate office of Donald
Downey, "an American in Paris" whom Sturges described as
a man "who sat up nights figuring out ways to rent vile apart-
ments without any windows in them ... by showing them at
night probably ... to pathetic young mothers, scarcely more
than children themselves. "[7] By the second or third day, the
result of the cold water bath that first night gave little Preston pneumonia, and a helpless Mary repented in guilt for her
son's life. Meanwhile, Isadora's mother, who would sometimes
care for Preston when Mary and Isadora wandered about in
pursuit of artistic expression, provided her own remedy, ad-
ministering a spoonful of champagne to the baby every few
hours. The next morning little Preston was cured--albeit
crocked. "This seems an unusual treatment for an infant,"
Sturges noted, "but it is clearly stated on page 27 in Mother's
book ... so it must be true. "[8]

That first year in Paris was a poetic transcription of
daily life for Mary. She wrote in her memoirs:[9]

> Here Monet and his family lived in an old-fashioned
> garden, adjoining the Moulin Rouge, our home.
> Frederic MacMonnies, the famous sculptor, also
> had a lovely place nearby, and we all lived the
> beautiful, simple, French life. I remember one
> Easter Sunday when we climbed high in the hills
> and sat all day and listened to Isadora read Shake-
> speare and Shelley. Here was nothing but beauty
> and innocence.

She continued about their idyll:[10]

> Parisian society in those days was like a fairy tale
> ... Carrière or Besnard would take us on a Sunday
> morning with a group of their children through the
> Louvre or Luxembourg museum, pointing out to us
> the beauty of the works of the great masters. Af-
> terwards we would all go to their homes to eat the
> simplest of repasts, glowing with happiness.

This experience undoubtedly sounds too rapturous to
be true. But Mary's reminiscences remain focused on the
pleasure of this pursuit of an exalted art. "At this time
Isadora knew nothing of love or lovers and I don't think the
question of sex was ever mentioned between us," wrote Mary.
"All was study and hard work. Isadora was to me like a
beautiful flower, exquisite and fragile, whose only thought was
her art."[11]

After more than a year abroad, Mary returned to America and accepted a marriage proposal from an old beau, Solomon Sturges, whose appearance in her life was indeed fortui-
tous and provided her with one of the most reliable relationships she ever had--and young Preston with the only man he
ever recognized as a father. Solomon was descended from
one of Chicago's most prominent families, comprised of social leaders and great wealth, and was a successful stock-
broker, an accomplished athlete (an ex-bicycle champion of
Illinois--"on the high bicycle, of course"), and a devoted
father to Preston. In January 1902, when Preston was three,
Solomon adopted him and Preston's surname became Sturges.

Young Preston adored Solomon, his independence and
enterprising character. Solomon stood, and with comparable
force, diametrically opposite to Mary and her bohemianism,
and in him Preston found a man of total heart and generosity,

a figure of exemplary honor, and one who had the stability
and common sense lacking in life with his mother. In Solo-
man, Preston would grow to find the pragmatism of a decidedly American identity, free of the onerous obligations of attending the opera, going to museums, and being available to
Isadora and her coterie. Here, at least, he was to learn,
Chicago could afford him the amenities of gentlemen's clubs
and tailors, and of status as "Solomon Sturges' son. "

Early in their marriage, Solomon agreed to allow
Mary and the baby to spend six months a year in Europe
and six months in Chicago, and the arrangement worked
for a while. During one of these sojourns, Mary and Isadora reunited in Paris where Isadora was incorporating the
splendor of ancient Greece into her dance and dress. Attired in flowing white robes and in bare feet, Isadora easily
persuaded Mary to dress the same, and Mary, in turn, decided that little Preston should not be denied this external
sign of the beauty of antiquity. "What will you do in Chicago
with the cold lake winds?" Solomon asked. It would not
matter, Mary replied, for she had adopted these clothes for
life. [12] So, on their return to Chicago, attired in his Grecian tunic and sandals, little Preston was sent to school in
what, to his gleefully derisive young classmates, appeared
to be a little white dress.

By the time Preston was almost eight, the six months
of stultifying evenings by the fire with Solomon and the ut-
terly predictable social activity of Chicago drove Mary to
suggest that perhaps eleven months in Europe and one in
Chicago would be more tolerable. The discussion ended with
a recognition that the marriage had too. Mary awakened
Preston that night, with Solomon a bit drunk at her side,
and said, "Mother is going to live in Paris, darling, and
Father is going to stay here in Chicago. What do you want
to do?"[13]

Preston didn't hesitate: the man "whose unfailing
tenderness and gentleness ... extended back into the diffused
twilight before memory began" was the man with whom he
wanted to be. Then Solomon told him that he was not his
natural father. "I looked at him in stupefaction for a moment, then at my mother to see if he was joking, then back
at Father. Then I started to cry, " Sturges recalled late in
his life. "I know the kind of crying it was because I've seen
my own little boys cry that way when they are broken-hearted,
and after a while the intake of breath makes a gasping, hollow
sound more distressing than the crying itself. "[14]

Chicago, 1904. Preston Sturges in his Grecian tunic with his mother, Mary Desti.

Preston came to trust Solomon again, for he never stopped loving him. And even though he still wished to remain with him after this discovery, Mary took him to Paris with her.

"Time passes very slowly for lifers and small boys," reminisced Sturges about his French childhood, "and I seem to remember that at 61 Rue de Paris in Joinville-le-Pont, it came to a complete stop."[15] Several years earlier, Mary, compelled to more travels with Isadora, deposited little Preston with a Monsieur Rousseau and his family, and he stayed there so long that he came to believe Monsieur Rousseau was his father, Madame his mother, and their little boy, Dede, his brother. "We had a lovely house in which I helped Papa make his own shells for the shotgun with which he shot seagulls. We also preserved a large quantity of seasnakes in alcohol and formaldehyde and then sealed them in big jars. Why, I don't know, unless they were used in the very large school called La Parangon that his father, Doctor Rousseau, had next door to where we lived."[16] Mary and Isadora briefly parted company, and Mary finally retrieved her son and decided they should return to Paris.

Mary and Isadora's artistic zeal and accession to impulse continued over the next few years, during the rest of Preston's childhood, and up to the first world war. Some summers were spent in Bayreuth, and any time Mary and Isadora felt inspired to run off somewhere, there was always Mrs. Duncan or a responsible innkeeper and his family to look after Preston and Isadora's niece, Temple. Little Preston adjusted to their carefree and sometimes reckless style. The impact of such adult behavior on a little boy is inscrutable; the adventures, however, are not. When Isadora decided, for instance, that she and Mary needed the invigoration of the sea air toward the end of their summer in Bayreuth in 1904, she, her lover at the time (referred to as "Romeo" in Mary's memoirs), and Mary took the children to a tiny island off the coast of Helgoland for the day. The trip was so exhilarating that Isadora and Mary decided to stay there a few days more. Leaving the children on the island with an innkeeper and his wife, they returned to Helgoland for their baggage and to see Romeo off. Isadora decided to delay their trip back for one last evening with Romeo. A sudden storm raged; the villagers, referring to the inn on the island, said, "Maybe the hotel will stand." Frantic, Mary and Isadora were determined to return for the children immediately,

Bayreuth, 1904. Isadora Duncan (seated), with her niece, Temple, and Mary Desti.

though everyone thought the choppy waves would capsize any small boat, that an attempted crossing would surely be a death mission. Now, the flair possessed by these two women acquired heroic dimensions: they got a boat and commandeered someone to row them back to the island. They found the children there, alive, drenched and frightened, but well, and after their rescue that night, they were given hot tea and whiskey and put to bed.

At this time, Isadora, as if commissioned by a greater countenance, mandated that Mary wed Von Bary the opera tenor and their amused and jovial companion. Neither was keen on the idea and it was one of the few times Mary suspected Isadora's judgment. "I remember something about going to the state opera in Dresden, " Sturges said, "because I had to catch up on my sleep by taking naps in the afternoon instead of playing in the municipal gardens with the other children and this poisoned my existence. The operas I liked were <u>The Flying Dutchman</u>, I liked the Spinning Song and the water scenes, and Samson and Delilah, because I always hoped the columns were going to hit Von Bary on the head when he shook them down. I think they did one night but I'm not sufficiently certain of this to be truly happy about it."17

Preston was almost nine and inevitably bound for some sort of formal education because "the next thing I knew," he wrote, "large quantities of haberdashery and clothing started to be assembled and I started getting the kind of talks it was felt would prepare me for incarceration in a large French school."18 The trip back was a farce of deceit and misadventure. Almost broke, Mary was telling "the usual lies" about Preston's age to a doubtful purser who remarked that the little boy looked rather large for under six.

"Are you daring to presume to doubt my word?" challenged Mary.

The purser apologized. "But being a rat," Sturges recalled, "he came up to me presently ... and said with a very sweet smile:19

> 'My! What a fine big boy you are for under six yet!' And I said: 'Who is? Me? I'm going on nine'! With a triumphant leer he exclaimed, 'Ah hah! Just as I suspected! Nun also!' and hot-footed it down to Mother's cabin; but by the time she got through with him he was sorry the idea ever entered his head. Beginning with some re-marks about Germans in general, she passed lightly over boastful little idiots pretending to be older than they are, warmed to her subject about chivalry through the ages ... then let him have the Ab-Princess of Meiningen and her celebrated brother, the Kaiser, and what they would do to him through both barrels. One had the feeling by the time she finished that the Kaiser and his sis-ter used to drop in on us for lunch at least a couple of times a week.

"It was on this trip I believe that, wishing to give a theatrical performance, I invented a method called 'narratage' for which I got a gold medal and many compliments some twenty-five years later," Sturges further recalled.20 [See screenwriting section. --Author]

Having chosen 'Little Miss Muffet' as a down-to-
earth scenario apt to please everybody, being full
of sex, suspense and surprise, I placed a little
girl passenger on a tuffet, shoved a bowl of curds
and whey (or as close an approximation as the
deck steward could provide) into her clumsy little
hands, and had my mother read this deathless poem
in her finest pear-shaped tones. While she read,
her son, remarkably disguised as a spider by the
superimposition of a green veil that covered him
like a tent, appeared hissing from behind a sofa,
leapt upon the little girl violently, knocked her off
her tuffet, stepped in the curds and whey, then
chased her, screaming out of the main saloon. I
need hardly add that the play was an immense success.

Preston was enrolled first as a day student and later
as a boarder at La Petite Ecole, the small boys' half of the
well-known Paris Lycée Janson-de-Sailly. He was later
transferred to schools in Normandy and then in Switzerland
when doctors diagnosed a tiny spot on his lung as tuberculo-
sis. Here, he excelled in athletics, especially soccer, boxing, and boating, and practiced the violin--terribly. Meanwhile, Mary found a compelling attraction to Aleister Crowley, one of the legendary satanists of modern time and a
great user of all his disciples. Preston accompanied them
to Italy during his vacation from school the summer he turned
twelve, after Mary and Crowley had searched tirelessly for
the right villa--the only villa--upon which to consecrate the
sacred temple of Crowley's magical spiritualism. Under her
new name of Soror Virakam, Mary was to transcribe the dic-
tation of Crowley's Book 4 of The Great Work--not, however,
before locating "the temple. " And when they stumbled upon
4-1-8 Villa Caldarazzo (418 being the number of the Magical
Formula of Aeon, a numerical hieroglyph of The Great Work),
they were elated. Preston, however, found it cold, damp,
and with leaky plumbing, and was eager to return to Switzerland.

Crowley disliked Preston. Preston loathed him. In
The Great Work, Crowley refers to him as "the brat, " but
"compared to what I always referred to him as, " Sturges
wrote, "it is a compliment. "[21] Among the features Preston
particularly loathed about this "phonus bolonus" was Crowley's
skull, completely shaved except for "one small tufted square
in the middle of his cranium. " Here, he "promenaded his

fingers as if they were dogs one has taken out to water. "
One of the more revolting practices he performed with imposing solemnity was incising his raised forearm with a
long, thin stiletto every time Mary used the singular personal pronoun, "I," "me," or "mine," instead of the mandated first person plural, "we," "us," and "ours. "

Sturges summed up the experience of his mother's
involvement with this "prophet":[22]

> Generally accepted as one of the most depraved,
> vicious and revolting humbugs that ever escaped
> from a nightmare or a lunatic asylum, the prac-
> titioner and staunch defender of every form of vice
> historically known to man, universally despised and
> enthusiastically expelled from every country he tried
> to live in, Mr. Crowley was nevertheless consid-
> ered by my mother to be not only the epitome of
> charm and good manners, but also the possessor
> of one of the very few brains she had been privi-
> leged to observe during her entire lifetime, that
> she could almost bring herself to admire. Ask me
> not why! It is possible of course that at this time,
> around 1910, Mr. Crowley had not yet attained the
> full flower of his later perfection. Rereading some
> of his subsequent exploits, I realize that my mother
> and I were lucky to escape with our lives. If I
> had been a little older he might not have escaped
> with his.

Mary and Aleister Crowley soon parted. Mary, having
tried every religion she encountered, must finally have seen
the spiritual limitations of his.

Under the mistaken impression that he was a wealthy banker,
Mary encouraged the attentions of Vely Bey Denizli, a son of
Ilias Pasha who was attending physician to Abdul Hamid, the
last Sultan of Turkey. His family, widely respected in his
country, also had the dubious distinction of having been tu-
tored by Basil Zaharoff, later to become one of the leading
international arms brokers. Vely, however, was not wealthy
and mistakenly thought Mary was (perhaps because of her use
of the Sturges name, which became frequent when she needed
to get out of a jam). They married, only to discover the
truth about each other.

Sturges Suit Blamed to Art
Wife to Acquiesce in Decree

Mrs. Solomon Sturges in her Grecian dress adapted from that of Isadora Duncan, of whose art Mrs. Sturges was a patron.

Devotion of _____ and Writer to Different Ideals Is Called Cause of Estrangement.

JAN 25 1911

The love of Mrs. Mary d'Salm Sturges, wife of Solomon Sturges, nephew Chicago, and head of the brokerage firm of Solomon Sturges & Co., for all forms of art, and especially for that form of revelation in dancing which Isadora Duncan is the century's greatest exponent, is blamed by friends of both Mr. and Mrs. Sturges for the marital differences that led to the filing of a suit for divorce by Mr. Sturges in Chicago last Monday.

It was some years ago that Mrs. Sturges, a woman of intellectual accomplishments and an enthusiast in whatever she undertakes, became interested in the dancing of Isadora Duncan. The teachings of Miss Duncan made a deep impression upon the mind of Mrs. Sturges. She became an exponent of the Duncan style of dancing and dress, but she differed from the Duncan in this respect. While Isadora Duncan advocated the use of the classic flowing Grecian draperies for dress on the stage, Mrs. Sturges was content to adopt it because she only as a tribute to the aestheticism. She was perfectly willing to appear at social functions and on the street in the ordinary garb of the woman of to-day. In her own home, however, she was always demanding something in the Grecian way.

As one friend expressed it yesterday, "Mrs. Sturges was wedded to her art and Mr. Sturges was wedded to the thirty hats in his office, they would have been amicable."

When the divorce suit of Mr. Sturges is called his wife, it is said, will be represented by counsel and will make a formal denial of the charge of desertion, but she will not, in fact, aid her husband in procuring it.

"As counsel of Mr. Fate, where she has appealed the said part of her flag in the domestic difficulties, Mrs. Sturges still hopes to win her husband, the said, to her side of her case," declared Mr. Paul her counsel.

But Mary also discovered something else. Vely, it turned out, possessed the formula for an antiwrinkle beauty compound invented by his father and kept in the family. She immediately saw the fortune to be made from marketing what she would call "The Secret of the Harem," so, in 1911, she opened her famous cosmetics salon at 4 Rue de la Paix and named it "Maison d'Este." Paul Poiret fashioned the interior for her and Mary designed delicate lotion and perfume bottles and had them hand blown in Venice.

The opening of Maison d'Este was one of the society events of Paris, attended by many of the haute monde and cultural celebrities of the day. Isadora barely tolerated Mary's involvement with this, a situation totally reinforcing her disdain for commerce. But commercial it was: Maison d'Este developed into a pace-setting business for the cosmetics industry with Mary's introduction of new pigments of face powder (until then, there were only three standard pigments-- rachel, ocher, and mauve), rouge, and lip rouge and encouragement of sales by promoting her philosophy of "expressing yourself" through the creative use of color. Monsieur Coty, then a hugely successful perfumer, offered her a quarter of his interest in the business for the rights to market her products under the Coty name, but Mary, demonstrating her exquisite business judgment, had the "robber" thrown out.

Mary and Isadora were still constant companions, Isadora now running a school which she toured extensively. Young Preston would visit the studio in Neuilly, distracting the young dancers from their rehearsing, their required reading of Goethe, Schiller, and Rousseau, or their sessions of listening to Bach and Brahms, with a tango or a rag, much to Isadora's annoyance. Paris Singer--"Uncle Mun"-- the sewing machine heir and father of one of Isadora's children, was like a second father to Preston and always generous with spending money and his beautiful home at 1 Place des Vosges in Paris. When a family dispute erupted into an altercation between Preston and Vely one day, Paris asked Preston when he retreated to his home: "Where did you hit him?"

"On the nose," Preston replied.

Opposite: The Chicago Examiner, January 25, 1911. Mary Desti and Solomon finally divorce.

"That's where you made your mistake ... you should always hit a fat man in the stomach!" Paris advised.[23]

After the opening of Maison d'Este, the French branch of the Italian family demanded Mary's disassociation from the d'Este name, despite her rages that she was one of their line. With the threat of legal action hanging over her head, she reluctantly changed her name from d'Este, henceforth to be known as 'Desti. "

Her success in Paris made, Mary expanded Desti cosmetics with branches in Deauville, London, and finally New York. In fact, after the war and through the early 1920s, her beauty advice appeared in columns she wrote for newspapers like London's The Daily Sketch--articles titled "The Beauty That Is Skin Deep," "Are Beauties Ever Natural?," "Are Women Worthy of Fashion Freedom?," and probably one of particular interest, "Women's Beauty at Forty: Maturity More Charming Than Girlhood. "

In 1913-14, Preston was attending La Villa, a boys' boarding school in Lausanne. He had spent a couple of earlier summers learning the Desti business and when, in the summer of 1914 as he approached sixteen, Mary asked him to run the Deauville branch, he was thrilled. He could draw well and started out by designing the advertising posters.

Early Years and Early Successes and Failures and Successes ...

Deauville was one of the nicest experiences of Preston's youth. It was the resort's opening season and, here, he was in full charge of the Maison Desti which Mary had housed in the same building as the world-famous restaurant, Ciro's. She had, in fact, arranged to take a shop on the main floor of the building, as Ciro's was on the second, and have thrown into the package a room and bath for Preston on the third floor and all his meals free at the restaurant. Every morning at five thirty, he would put on old clothes and go downstairs with morning coffee and a croissant to sweep, clean, and polish the shop. Then he would go back upstairs to bed. "At ten thirty I came down again," he said, "but this time officially, wondrously decked out in white flannel trousers with brown and white shoes, a tan gabardine jacket with a belt in the back, and a carnation in my buttonhole. Having assured myself, by running a suspicious finger across the shelves, that the night porter had done his work sufficiently, I would retire to Ciro's for an exotic breakfast."[24]

Deauville exposed him to the glamorous and fashionable, and to the wealthy, and not as a boy with his mother this time, but as a young businessman. "Billionaires were ten cents a dozen, and the beach and the casino and the racetrack were crawling with dukes, barons, ex-kings, maharajahs, gigolos, politicians, newspaper owners, Rothschilds, gigolos, opera stars, generals, gigolos...."[25] Preston recognized many of them when they came into the shop: Jules Bache, the banker and Mary's friend, the ballroom team of Maurice and Florence Walton, Elsie Janis, Irene Bordoni, Ted Sloan, Kid McCoy and Frank Moran, the world heavyweight title contender, "and some of the boatriders from the New York Bar [who] would come down for the weekend. (In case you are from the country, a boatrider plays cards on boats and wins.)"[26]

By now, Mary's marriage to Vely Bey had soured. Prone to fury, Vely threatened murder and suicide out of love for her and exasperation at the capriciousness that made life with Mary impossible. One afternoon in Paris, he entered her room, locked the door behind him, and announced that he was going to kill her. "She didn't get too frightened," Sturges recalled, "having had some experience along those lines with Mr. Biden and his revolver."[27] They survived each other one more time, and in a union that was originally remarkable for maintaining the volatile temperaments of both.

Preston never finished school after that summer in Deauville. The war started in August and the summer revelers fled Deauville in any conveyance available--train, automobile, cart--and Mary was relieved to see him back and safe in Paris. Passionate about creating support for the war relief, Mary tried to establish a hospital in Paris, much to the annoyance of Ambassador Myron Herrick. Herrick assured her that this was only a minor war, that it certainly had nothing to do with American women living in Paris and was no cause for patriotic hysteria. Mary was outraged; but what she failed to realize at this point was that, in marrying Vely, she had automatically lost her American citizenship. And when Turkey joined Germany in the war, she became by definition an enemy alien. When this became known, mobs stormed into Maison Desti, broke bottles and jars, and threw furniture out the windows. Mary had escaped to Deauville where she eventually did open her hospital.

War made it fearfully apparent, too, that before long the young men who didn't enlist would be conscripted. Apprehensive, Mary had Preston return to Deauville, fill a trunk with as many Desti products as possible, and sail for New York. And New York was but a stone's throw from Chicago, where Preston rushed to see his father for the first time since he was a little boy. Upon seeing him at Union Station, he ran over to Solomon and kissed him on both cheeks. "This amused my father very much," Sturges recalled, "and the next time I came to Chicago, having learned the American style of not kissing your father, he grabbed me in his arms, kissed me on both cheeks and said: 'I've been saving that for you.'"28

A few months later, Mary arrived in New York. The cosmetics business was losing money because of the war, and, taking some bad financial advice, she filed for bankruptcy. It was a move she regretted the rest of her life. Just when things looked bleakest, Isadora and all her girls followed to New York and life picked up again. Mary moved in with her into a large suite at the Ritz; a studio opened up on the corner of Fourth Avenue and Twenty-Third Street, complete with Isadora's old faded blue drapes and Steinway concert grand piano; and the usual Duncan coterie flocked around--a coterie that included painters, poets, stage designers, musicians, and, especially to the delight of Preston with his burgeoning interest in photography, Arnold Genthe, Edward Steichen, and Alfred Stieglitz.29

Isadora was preparing to mount her production of Oedipus Rex at the Century Theatre with her brother Augustin as Oedipus, and offered sixteen-year-old Preston his first theatre job as an assistant stage manager. His function was to cue the lighting and sound technicians when to produce lightning and thunder after Oedipus returns on stage to deliver his big monologue upon having blinded himself. Preston was to flash a green light for lightning, followed by a red one for thunder. The obvious confusion followed. "The first time Gus staggered on stage," described Sturges, "the thunder crashed down on him from the flys, he looked over toward me in startled fury, then tried to shout it down, but all the audience saw was a man waving his arms and all they heard was my thunder."30 Oedipus ran for a while, Isadora moving it from theatre to theatre because of fire restrictions or the expensive tickets which she saw as a deliberate denial of art to the people. She finally moved the production to Jacob Adler's Yiddish Theatre on Avenue B, where tickets sold for ten cents a seat--the best going to scalpers, who undoubtedly made a killing during the run. Preston would have no further involvement with the theatre until long after the war.

Mary had reopened the Desti emporium by now in a small shop at 23 East Ninth Street. It lacked the elegance of Paul Poiret's decor and of the hand-blown crystal, but the raw materials needed to recreate some of the products were available, and the New York bottle and label wholesalers provided a respectable version of the now defunct European Maisons Desti. ("'The Secret of the Harem' was now called 'Youth Lotion' because the Turks had gone over to the side of Germany.")[31] About this time, Vely Bey came to New York to visit Mary and Preston and to market a scheme for a paperless cigarette (a tobacco leaf was healthier). Isadora, on the other hand, was preparing to return her troupe to Europe; most of her young dancers were German and the war was making them increasingly patriotic, and Isadora was proally. Mary and Preston went to the boat to see her off. Vely, who never liked Isadora and held her partly responsible for his marital problems with Mary, came along. Everyone, from the cast and crew of Oedipus to noted artists and celebrities, was there. It was such an emotional and tearful farewell that when Isadora called to Mary--"If you don't come with me, I don't know what I'll do!"--Mary took her cue.

"You aren't going to fall for anything that stupid, are you?" Vely asked with amazement.

"You don't understand," Mary said, taking Preston in her arms. 'Do what you can, darling! Keep things going! I'll send you some money as soon as I can!"[32]

Preston and Vely found themselves waving goodbye to them both. They also kept the Desti business going while it made just enough money to keep its doors open. But Vely, seeing no way to make a profit, felt that Maison Desti should close. Preston felt otherwise, and Vely left him the business to run alone. "Now, then, for the first time," wrote Alexander King of Sturges during this period, "the young genius was ready to make his initial assault on that stony façade where neither Duncan drapes nor Desti dreams could hide the drying blood of other hopeful assailants."[33]

About two months after Mary left--in July 1915--Preston received an incredible cable from her informing him that J.P. Morgan and Company, through Morgan, Harjes and Company in Paris, had two thousand dollars waiting for him to keep the Desti business running and for advertising. By a stroke of good fortune, Mary ran into Mrs. Harold McCormick, the daughter of John D. Rockefeller, in Zurich and convinced herself in typical fashion (after the third effort, it became "an absolutely positive certainty beyond the faintest peradventure of a doubt")[34] that the two must have known each other well back in Chicago. Edith McCormick came to Isadora's rescue when she and her German dancers were stranded in Switzerland, and now extended her generosity to the tune of ten thousand dollars to help poor Mary--not Mary Desti, but Mary Sturges of the Chicago Sturgeses--out of her financial bind. The loan, a godsend, kept the Desti emporium solvent for some time.

Meanwhile, in New York, Preston continued the operation of the small retail concern. The Desti business taught him about mixing preparations, packaging and marketing them. "All sorts of people came into the shop," he said, "and the better known they were, the nicer they were."[35] Lillian Russell, Mae Marsh, and young Peggy Guggenheim came in; so did Hamilton Fish and Madame Charles J. Walker, the first black millionairess, famous for marketing the first hair-straightening process.

In the fall of 1916, Preston left the cosmetics business to become a runner on Wall Street in an attempt to earn the minimum ten dollars weekly that would qualify him for enlistment in the air service. The air service refused young men who wanted to join up with them to make the better money by imposing this restriction. Preston came to envision a potential future on Wall Street modeled much after his father's success. Solomon, who didn't think much of the idea and never thought of himself as essentially "anything but a betting commissioner,"[36] was so persuaded by Preston that he got him a runner's job for seven dollars a week at F.B. Keech and Company, associates of his Chicago firm. His one big coup during his brief excursion into Wall Street finance came when Paris Singer helped him out by buying twenty-thousand dollars' worth of stocks. That sale immediately raised his weekly salary to ten dollars. The footwork was exhausting though, with Preston literally running as many as twenty-four deliveries a day in the area before realizing that the brokerage business held no future for him.

In April 1917, America declared war against Germany
and Preston was eager to enlist. A blind spot in one eye
kept him out of the air service, but Mary, using the Sturges
name, managed to make such a fuss over the matter with a
major general who was from Chicago that Washington decided
Preston's blind spot wasn't as critical as they had thought.
He was accepted by the air service in July, sent to Camp
Dick in Texas, and graduated in the Sixty-Third Squadron.
Spyros Skouras, who would figure in his later film career
at Fox, was a barracks mate and fellow graduate. At Camp
Dick, he published his first piece of writing; at the request
of the editor, Preston wrote "300 Words of Humor" for the
camp newspaper.

At dinner one evening at the University Club in Chicago, Solomon asked him what his plans were upon being dis-
charged. Preston had no idea. "I thought I had some talent
for mechanics, having just invented and drawn up a multiple
speed planetary gear arrangement for automobiles," he said,
"although I just discovered that Louis Chevrolet had patented
the same idea in 1900 ... but that only proved I was in the
right direction."[37] Solomon asked why he didn't go to Hollywood and "engage in the motion picture business which seemed
to be developing into something quite solid and respectable."

"You mean as an actor?" Preston said in horror.

"Of course not!" said Solomon, who never met an
actor he liked. "I mean in the business end of the ...
business, or whatever you call it."

"I wouldn't know just how to start," Preston replied.
Solomon suggested that they talk further about it in the future.[38]

Mary lost track of Vely during most of the war, and one day
she began to think he might well be dead. Having thought
this long enough, a few days later she was convinced it was
so, and was "absolutely certain of it by the end of the month,
at which time, bearing up courageously under her widowhood,
she married a young Englishman."[39] Madame Desti now became Madame Edward Perch--on occasion. And soon after
the wedding, she persuaded her new husband that Preston
should come to Paris to be with his mother. Mary, who re-
tained much of her youthful beauty and always referred to
Preston as her "baby," faced the rather embarrassing mo-

ment, at the train station one morning at three o'clock, of introducing a fully grown son to his new, startled, and not much older stepfather.

Maison Desti suffered during the war and, after the service and a brief return to Keech, Preston returned to build it up. With a keen interest in inventing, he created new cosmetics compounds for the Desti line and a kissproof lipstick with a vanishing cream base that almost alone kept Desti going into the 1920s. Mary, too, had pulled off one of her more audacious feats when she asked Morgan, Harjes for the additional francs she felt were owed to her on the Edith McCormick loan now that the franc was devalued at a rate of twenty-eight to the dollar. When she borrowed the ten thousand dollars, the rate of exchange was five to one, but as she hadn't yet paid it back, the account was still open and she insisted on the difference of 230,000 francs. Much to Morgan, Harjes' exasperation, Mary was paid them.

In 1920, Preston closed the retail beauty business and opened a warehouse in Brooklyn to manufacture the Desti products for wholesale marketing. Being a small business-man gave him the sense of definition and responsibility he wanted, and even enabled him to pursue his inventions. He married Estelle de Wolfe Mudge of Bristol, Rhode Island, a well-off socialite, in December 1923, and the two of them lived in the country while he perfected his inventions and tried to patent them. Preston loved gadgets--almost as much as Solomon despised them--and worked on projects such as a vertical flight control that enabled a plane to fly up and down, to hover and land easily; a bantam automobile with the engine in the rear; an automatic oiler for automobile springs; a process of intaglio photoengraving; and a library filing system.

During this time, Mary was facing her own downturn. The Desti shops in Europe were closing, her beauty column stopped being published, and she was chronically out of mon-ey. In a move that left the newly married Preston hurt and disillusioned, Mary, back from Europe again in 1923, took back what he was under the impression she had given him back in 1915: she took back the Desti emporium in New York, all except the rights and profits to his kissproof lip-stick. Preston pleaded with her to stay away long enough so that he could "do it on my own."40 But Mary wouldn't yield, and the loss of Maison Desti estranged him from his mother. The following year, Mary reopened the retail business and ran it in her usual haphazard manner.

Preston's life as a country gentleman and inventor put
a strain on his marriage, whose sole financial support during
its last year was his wife's assured income.   "His fevered
elucidations made to prospective investors were mingled,"
commented Alexander King, "with the echoes of their departing footsteps."[41]   After three years of marriage, Preston
and Estelle were divorced in 1927.   Depressed by his divorce,
no challenges or inspiration seemed worth his pursuit.   Mary
and Solomon became concerned about his desolation, and Mary
attempted to allay his despair by returning Maison Desti to him.
Solomon even invested in it.   But the business didn't do much
better than it had under his mother, and Mary, now back in
Paris, was always cabling for money.   Paris Singer wrote to
Preston on July 5, 1927:[42]

> I have seen your mother and she says she is
> getting ready to give you 'what for'! ! ! ! !
> I told her you had everything well in hand and
> she said she knew it, especially the cash and that
> she could not live on broken promises and your
> neglect.
> I of course took your part and explained at once
> that your expenses were immense....   This did
> not seem to deter her from her desire to meet you
> shortly.

Maison Desti finally had to close.   Preston was twenty-
nine and a young man without profession or vocation, and
worse--without the pride of personal, creative, accomplishment.

Mary, still in Europe in the fall of 1927, was devastated and deeply depressed: in September, Isadora died in
Nice.   The fringe of the long shawl wrapped around her
neck--"the shawl she had taken away from me"--caught in
the wheels of the moving Bugatti she rode, each revolution
of the wheel pulling the shawl tighter and tighter, and she
was instantly strangled.   Mary wrote to Preston on October
31st:[43]

> Preston darling--
>
> You will understand why I haven't written.   The
> shock has been too awful.   I put Isadora in the
> car, and before she had gone five yards, I called
> to her that her shawl was dragging--suddenly they
> stopped--I thought because I had called about the

shawl, but really because the chauffeur saw that
her dear head was drawn beside her knees.

Her grief over Isadora's death was the second, final, ironic
connection between life and death that they shared.   Fourteen
years earlier, when Isadora's children were taken for an
outing, young Preston was originally to be with them.   However, he misbehaved the day before and Mary punished him
by not allowing him to go.   The following day the chauffeured
car in which Isadora's small children and their nurse were
riding slid into the Seine, and the children and their nurse
drowned inside the car.   The bizarre circumstances of Isadora's own death in Nice by the constriction of Mary's shawl
jarred Mary into a state of deteriorating health from which
she would never recover.

Early in 1927, Preston had very nearly recovered his
joie de vivre and went to visit Solomon in Chicago for the
Christmas holidays.   Purposely dressed in a shabby suit to
evoke his father's sympathy, Preston's appearance so affected Solomon that he sent him to his tailor to be outfitted
for new clothes.   While he was being measured, he doubled
over in pain.   His appendicitis was misdiagnosed at first,
and that nearly cost him his life when his appendix burst
and he developed peritonitis; but after a six-week recovery
at Presbyterian Hospital, Preston was released.   His re-
cuperation at his father's apartment provided him with the
time to consider writing--a musical revue--in an endeavor
that would change the course of his creative future.

Sturges the Playwright

Preston's decision to write a play came with no previous
encouragement from the theatre.   His only source for the
craft of playwrighting was the rather arbitrary choice of
Brander Matthews' book, A Study of the Drama, which Solomon brought to him in the hospital.   Matthews' book provided
him with a clear and useful handbook for structuring his plays
and it remained for Preston a far more valuable tool for dramatic technique than the abstract and ultimate envisionings of
the theatre described by Isadora and Mary's friend and sometime mentor, Gordon Craig.   To Preston, his hospital experience was loaded with the comic implications of healing the
sick and of surgical procedures, and out of it came the inspiration for a musical revue based on Irvin S. Cobb's

short book of humor, Speaking of Operations. Cobb, in fact, hearing of Preston's idea, wrote to him on February 23, 1928, that he would indeed like to collaborate with him on this, Preston's first play. [44]

Speaking of Operations was finished but, alas, put aside as an unfunny product of anesthesia. Preston's musical career can be summed up as a creative anomaly. When he was thirteen, he composed a little rag called "Winky" in honor of his affection for Elsie Janis. It was mistakenly thought by a music publisher in Latvia to represent the current popular American music and was subsequently published to popular success there. Later, in New York, Preston was to acquire a hasty and rather dubious musical education through answering an advertisement for a sit-down-and-play-at-once course in piano playing offered by "Piano Bill" for one dollar. He learned to play according to a system that did not require the learning of notes. Later in Preston's career, Ted Snyder, the composer, gave him instruction, noting that Preston had a talent for writing short sentences. Snyder taught him the concept of "wedding the words and the music." However, music publishers, after listening to his songs, told him to relinquish any musical aspirations. Snyder and Preston, however, did publish one song together, "My Cradle of Dreams"; and Preston published some of his own songs in 1928, among them, "Maybe You'll Be My Baby" and "Asia Minor Blues."

Mary was on her way to the Soviet Union after being in Chicago during Preston's hospitalization. T. R. Smith of Horace Liveright had been after her to write her memoirs of Isadora's last years, and, after some reluctance, she agreed. Isadora's school was still operating in Moscow and Mary was going there to do research and to arrange for the students to dance in America. In the introduction of The Untold Story: The Life of Isadora Duncan, 1921-27, Mary invoked her distinctive perception of the truth when she wrote: "... what is here written is the absolute truth and the last service I can render to the most loyal friend a woman ever had and a tribute to the greatest artist of her time."[45] In her finest lugubrious prose, Mary venerates the memory of Isadora:[46]

> When we arrived at the palace now used as Isadora's school, the great doors were thrown wide and pouring down the broad marble staircase came a hundred of Isadora's children, all attractively

dressed in red velvet tunics with narrow red velvet
bands about their hair. They looked like angels,
and the agony that took possession of me, that I
and not Isadora had come to see them, was beyond
endurance. Limp and helpless I leaned against the
balustrade as the children gathered about me, almost carrying me up to the stairs, making a speech
they had prepared before our arrival. Then they
cried, 'But, Mary, you look out of the eyes like
Isadora. You are like our Isadora. '

Sturges' first completed and produced full-length play
was The Guinea Pig, based on a cruel personal experience
of being misled by a young actress to believe that she found
him witty and charming, when actually she saw Sturges as
the exemplary bore of his social class. She told him during an
argument one night that he was being scrutinized for her dramatic research, and out of outrage, Sturges was provoked to
write a play himself--to prove not only that he could do it, but
that he could do it better than she. In less than two months
Sturges wrote The Guinea Pig: Broadway producers unanimously
rejected it. Consequently, it was rehearsed out of town and first
performed at the Wharf Players Theatre in Provincetown on July
30, 1928. Sturges borrowed money to get to Provincetown and
stage the production and was so much in the hole, despite
the play's short run, that he had to hock his watch to pay
his Provincetown landlady and get back to New York. The
Guinea Pig, however, attracted enough attention to reach
Broadway. It turned out that Sturges' gimmick of presenting
a winter opening in a summer theatre worked, and the Provincetown audiences loved it. Charles Abramson, the lawyer
turned producer, told Sturges over a late-night cup of coffee,
that $2500 was the absolute minimum required to produce the
play on Broadway. When Sturges came up with the money,
a very surprised Abramson agreed to put it on. Jack Gil-
christ would direct it and Alexander Carr would star. The
play ran for sixty-seven performances at the President Theatre on West Forty-Eighth Street and received good reviews.

After The Guinea Pig, Sturges went on the road as an
assistant stage manager for a couple of shows. One of them,
Hotbed, was closed by the police in Chicago, where Sturges
remained at his father's apartment to write his next play.
He sent a completed draft of it to Brock Pemberton, the
producer who hired him for the stage managing jobs, and
Pemberton liked Strictly Dishonorable. Sturges' play, a
light comedy about an Italian opera singer who captivates a

small-town girl engaged to someone else, was battled over between playwright and producer until it opened. They fought over everything, and when Strictly Dishonorable opened on September 9, 1929, Sturges was convinced that after the battering the production had sustained during rehearsals, it was destined to fail. He stayed away from the premiere, got drunk and went to bed, unaware of the delighted critics and audience who changed his life overnight.

Strictly Dishonorable, directed by Antoinette Perry, was nothing short of a smash hit and ran over sixty-four weeks on Broadway. It was often sold out and tickets went as high as twelve dollars when they could be found.

His next theatre projects immediately following Strictly Dishonorable were a play, Recapture, staged in New York in January 1930 with Melvyn Douglas, and an operetta called The Well of Romance, which he agreed to do with Maurice Jacquet--Jacquet composing the music and Sturges working on the lyrics and book. Both failed miserably. "The critics boiled me in oil and then danced a swan song on my corpse," Sturges wrote to Solomon about Recapture. [47]

After the success of Strictly Dishonorable, Sturges heard from Edmund Biden, his natural father, for the first time since infancy. Biden, remarried and the father of a baby, invited Sturges to dinner. "I went," Sturges said, "but sometime during the evening he said something rude about my mother, so I left and never saw him again during his lifetime although he became very anxious to see me after I became rich and well-known and things were going badly for him. But I never forgave him ... especially an insane and sadistically imaginative letter he wrote later expressing his great joy at my mother's death." [48]

"In 1930," Sturges recalled twenty-five years later, "I was at the Everglades Club and various places--including Colonel Bradley's gambling casino--helling around and romancing a very rich young girl I would have been far better off never to have married--her name was Hutton, I believe." [49] But Sturges did marry Edward Hutton's step-daughter, Eleanor, and not without overcoming the persistent opposition of her father. He described the ordeal in a letter to Solomon: [50]

> She liked me too and we wanted to get married on the 3rd of June.... The family promptly decided

that I was a fortune hunter, a bum, a drunkard,
and everything else they could think of to say.
Hutton had detectives put on my trail to dig me
up a bad reputation, if possible, but so far, they
haven't succeeded. They have promised to cut
Eleanor off without a cent if she marries me without their consent, and when I still wanted to marry
her, it knocked the fortune hunter theory for a loop.

"Those of us who knew him during that period remember him as a multi-lingual glamour boy of large proportions
and large gestures, who was, in the truest sense of the word,
happy," wrote Alexander King.[51] The tabloids had fun with
this image, too. Fond of frequenting dance halls, Sturges was
depicted as a celebrity playwright who married well yet enjoyed an insinuatingly compromising social life. (Eleanor was
then in Paris studying voice.) Yet Sturges wasn't unfaithful;
and to vindicate himself in the face of this reckless publicity,
he wrote his 1931 play, Child of Manhattan (originally titled
Consider the Lily, it was staged in 1932), as a kind of proof
of his pursuing, not women, but his craft. It ran briefly on
Broadway before being sold to the movies.

The terms of sale for dramatic properties to the movies in those days brought fifty per cent to the author and fifty
per cent to the producer. Producer A. C. Blumenthal--
"Blumey"--represented Sturges in the sale of Strictly Dishonorable and Child of Manhattan, and trapped him in a financial obligation that required Sturges to pay back a two-
thousand-dollar loan against the movie sale of Child of Manhattan. Sturges was on a ship returning from Paris, where
he went to pursue Eleanor, and was unable to meet the payment exactly on the specified date. Blumenthal refused late
payment. Consequently, Sturges was paid all of his money
for the movie sale of Strictly Dishonorable, but Blumenthal
took one hundred per cent of the money from the sale of
Child of Manhattan.

Sturges attempted to repair his fortune by writing more
for the movies. Originally, his screenwriting venture started
out as quite a financial lesson as well. He had written his
first screenplay, The Big Pond, for Paramount in two weeks
in 1929 and received two thousand dollars for it, only to
learn later that the average rate for scripts was ten weeks
at ten thousand dollars. He then wrote the dialogue for Paramount's Fast and Loose in 1930, while Universal was about
to film Strictly Dishonorable with the screenplay by Gladys

Lehman and John Stahl directing. After its release, Sturges wrote to Universal's president, Carl Laemmle, of his delight in the result. In November 1931, he heard from Laemmle:[52]

> Dear Mr. Sturges:
>
> WHAT STORY WITH SCREEN POSSIBILITIES DO YOU CONSIDER THE BEST YOU HAVE EVER WRITTEN? I don't care whether or not it has been published. It may have been lying in a trunk in the attic or in the cellar for years. It may have been the world over in magazines and book form....
> That such a story exists and that its title has already flashed through your mind I haven't the slightest doubt.... I would like to hear about that story, learn whether the film rights are for sale, and discuss its picture possibilities with you.
> It is understood, of course, that this favorite story of yours will, if accepted by us, be given the finest screen treatment our studio facilities can provide.
>
> Cordially,
> Carl Laemmle
> President

Preston and Eleanor Sturges had been married one year when, on their first anniversary in April 1931, Mary Desti died.

Eleanor returned to Paris to study voice. She never came back to New York, and, by the end of April 1932, the Sturges' marriage was over. In July, Paris Singer, "Uncle Mun," died.

A phase of Sturges' youthful life appeared at an end. In September of 1932, he went to California on commission by Universal to write the screenplay of H. G. Wells's The Invisible Man.

Early Hollywood Years

"Unlike other rebels against traditional studio smugness, he had the instant conviction that, despite their job-lot condition, the movies were the most vital theatrical factor in the world.

On this conviction," King wrote, "rests the claim that he has never stopped writing plays."[53] But Sturges' early distinction as a screenwriter became a veiled attempt to lift himself from the obscurity of precisely this job-lot condition to a position of recognition. His version of The Invisible Man, requested by Laemmle as a vehicle for Boris Karloff, was shelved and the extent to which any of it was finally used unclear. Universal did not renew Sturges' contract and he left in November 1932. Columbia released the film version of Child of Manhattan in February 1933, the script adapted by Gertrude Purcell and directed by Edward Buzzell. About the same time, Sturges sold The Power and the Glory, an original screenplay written solely by him, to Fox.

He wrote the part of Tom Garner in The Power and the Glory with Spencer Tracy in mind, and, in fact, the entire work was such a personal effort throughout the different stages of writing that when Sturges offered to sell Jesse Lasky, production head at Fox, a complete shooting script, Lasky was stunned to discover it required not a single change. He bought The Power and the Glory on Sturges' terms: for $17,500 plus a percentage of the picture's profits. The sale was a radical one and attracted much press notice that viewed with alarm the dangerous precedent of a writer being cut into the picture's gross and the threat to tradition in only a single writer doing an entire script. A particularly contentious article by B. P. Schulberg to the Hollywood Reporter, arguing the value of several writers on a script, so incensed Sturges that he replied in a letter to the editor:[54]

> After sending us his good wishes which we reciprocate, he unbosoms himself of the belief that from two to eight authors working on a single script are better than one. Now, if eight are better than one, eighty are better than eight, eight hundred are better than eighty, eight thousand are etc., etc. I for one can think of no surer way of stamping out originality, initiative, pride of achievement, and quality. You can't play football with a thought. The ideal talking picture would result from the alliance of painting, literature, and music. Considering these arts, no famous collaborations spring into the mind excepting, perhaps, the Bible. Barring a few sequences this would make a dull epic.

Furthermore, about the alleged inability of the same screenwriter to write both comedy and drama:

Sturges (seated) and director William K. Howard coaching young Cullen Johnston and Billy O'Brien in their lines for The Power and the Glory. (The Museum of Modern Art/ Film Stills Archive)

> Entirely apart from the fact that writers transmit emotions through words and that sad emotions are no more difficult to transmit than funny ones, there is the other fact that, without a sense of humor, a writer's sad scenes might easily become ludicrous and, without a sense of pathos, his funny scenes would not be very funny. Writers as double-jointed as all of this are: Shakespeare, Tolstoy, Noel Coward, Owen Davis, all of the Authors' League, and the members of the Writers' Club in Hollywood, to name but a few.

Fox released The Power and the Glory on August 18, 1933; it did modestly well at the box office but was critically recognized as a rare accomplishment in Hollywood filmmaking.

In 1934, Sturges wrote his fourth credited screenplay,

Thirty-Day Princess, for Paramount, starring Sylvia Sidney
and an early Cary Grant. At United Artists, Rouben Mamoulian, scheduled to direct Tolstoy's Resurrection as a star
vehicle for Samuel Goldwyn's new find, Anna Sten, wanted
Sturges and Maxwell Anderson to adapt the work. Sturges
wanted fifteen hundred dollars a week; Goldwyn grudgingly
agreed to it, but fired him after the project. Resurrection
was released as We Live Again on September 24th, flopped
at the box office, and practically terminated Sten's newly
launched career.

Two very successful pictures written by Sturges came
out in 1935. Diamond Jim, based on Parker Morrell's biography of railroad tycoon Jim Brady, was produced by Universal and, earlier in the year, William Wyler at Paramount
directed The Good Fairy, the adaptation of Ferenc Molnár's
play that Sturges wrote in late 1934. The studio, in fact,
anticipated such a critical and popular success with The Good
Fairy that it became the first picture ever booked at Radio
City Music Hall without a preview and backed up with advance
advertising solely on faith. 55 Sturges wrote the lyrics to Ted
Snyder's melody, "Paris in the Evening," used in the picture
The Gay Deception, and, in 1936, the lyrics for "Secret Ren-
dezvous," used in One Rainy Afternoon, United Artists' movie
based on Pressburger and Pujol's Monsieur sans Gêne.

In 1937, Paramount substantially distorted his script
for Hotel Haywire and, in July, put him on Cecil B. De-
Mille's project, The Buccaneer. In between the two, however, he was able to write his delightful screenplay Easy
Living, based on Vera Caspary's story and starring Jean
Arthur, Ray Milland, and Edward Arnold. Mitchell Leisen
directed it, but the film indelibly bears Sturges' signature.
The dizzying comedy and mad pace is, as Carl Laemmle
told him, "a brilliant job."56

But Sturges was becoming increasingly irritated with
the recurrent mishandling of his screenplays and was anxious
to write and direct his own material. Taking assignments
from studio to studio, perhaps he was at last beginning to
feel the job-lot condition he so effortlessly managed at first
but now saw as the chronic and rather ignominious treatment
of the screenwriter in the face of the movie industry machinery. He did some script work on Paramount's College
Swing before leaving for M-G-M in late 1937 to write a
version of Broadway Melody of 1939 and, later, the screenplay for Port of Seven Seas (with an uncredited Ernest Vajda),

based on Marcel Pagnol's Marseilles Trilogy. He returned
to Paramount in the spring of 1938 to adapt Justin Huntly
McCarthy's play about the exploits of François Villon, If I
Were King, and to work on Never Say Die, a vehicle for Bob
Hope and Martha Raye.

Remember the Night, written in 1939, was Sturges'
last script directed by someone else (Leisen again) and remains one of his finest screenplays.   The scenes, dialogue,
and the tone suffused throughout the story make the film un-
mistakably his and suggest, more clearly than ever, that
Sturges was a looming screen presence about to take new
shape.

Sturges never stopped inventing, and after he moved
to Hollywood he went into business with the designer Ivan Ad-
dison.   Together they opened the Sturges Engineering Company in Wilmington, California, in 1937.   Sturges' interest in
technology had grown since the war when he learned a little
about engines in the air service and found that Paris Singer
had a financial interest in them. [57]   At his engineering company, he designed and had built a vibrationless diesel engine
that he installed in the yacht he designed for himself.   During
World War II, Sturges Engineering would do subcontract work
for the navy.

Sturges married for the third time on November 7,
1938.   He and the former Louise Sargent Tevis would have
a son in June 1941, Solomon IV (Mon), named after Preston's
father.   Solomon Sturges and his second wife, Marie, bought
a house in Hollywood earlier in the year, but at the time of
Sturges' wedding in Nevada, Solomon was recovering from a
heart attack in Chicago.   His father moved to Los Angeles in
January 1939, where, a year later, in May 1940, he died.
"We never stopped loving each other," Sturges wrote, "and
he died in my arms in Hollywood, where he had come to be
near me at the end ... and I revere his memory."[58]

Riding the Crest in Hollywood: The Good Years

Sturges wrote the original screenplay for The Great
McGinty in 1933 under the title of The Biography of a Bum,
with Spencer Tracy in mind for the part of McGinty.   He
couldn't sell it then and five years later proposed it as a

magazine serial to The Saturday Evening Post. They weren't interested either. Now, in 1939, eager to prove that he could write and direct, Sturges persuaded William Le Baron, production head at Paramount, to give him the opportunity to direct. Le Baron had faith in Sturges and agreed to his giveaway offer to sell the screenplay of McGinty to the studio for one dollar in exchange for the chance to direct it. The legal department changed the price to ten dollars, to them a more legitimate figure. The production had a three-week shooting schedule and went through several title changes, from The Biography of a Bum to The Vagrant to Down Went McGinty and others, before finally being released as The Great McGinty on July 23, 1940.

The Great McGinty had absolutely nothing to assure box-office success. It had no star and consequently was not a vehicle; it was not a remake of an earlier favorite nor an adaptation of a popular novel or a play, and it had no sensational connection to a known living or historical person. As a political satire, McGinty had little more going for it than the creative thrust of its author-director. No small feat, it made The Great McGinty a sleeper hit, and rarely before had a picture made its director so well known.

A month later, J. P. McGowen of the Screen Directors' Guild asked Sturges to join. He declined, saying:[59]

> I want you to understand that I am deeply sensible to the honor you paid me ... and it is only because of a very deep conviction that guilds are principally useful to the lawyers whom they enrich that I must decline the invitation.
> It is the mode at the moment for everyone to belong to one union or subdivision of a union. Being so much out of fashion, I must seem very strange to you. I failed to make myself clear to my friends Mr. Frank Capra, Mr. Frank Lloyd, or Mr. William Wyler. Certainly also, I failed to make myself clear to my friends at the Screen Writers' Guild during the years in which I was overpowered by my desire not to join their organization. I am probably a little tetched in the haid, but that's how it is.
>
> Cordially yours,

A Cup of Coffee was a play Sturges wrote back in

1931; his screenplay version was successively titled Ants in Their Pants and The New Yorkers. A Cup of Coffee finally became Christmas in July, the second movie Sturges wrote and directed. After some bargaining, he got his old theatre friend, Alexander Carr, who had played a lead in The Guinea Pig and was by then a frequently unemployed actor, to play the department store owner, Mr. Schindel. And for Schindel's Department Store, Sturges invented the wonderful "Davenola," an all-service davenport-sleeper-lounger-bar-and-cabinet unit. After many casting possibilities, including a young William Holden, Dick Powell was chosen for the part of the lead, Jimmy MacDonald. The role was a far more demanding and intelligent variation of Powell's boy-next-door parts of the 1930s.

As much as The Great McGinty satirized the flaws and self-serving opportunities for unscrupulous behavior in the American political machinery, so did Christmas in July cast a skeptical look at the pursuit of recognition and fortune in a consumerist society. Both films made a refreshing impression on the public. Christmas in July came out in September of 1940 and, with The Great McGinty, enjoyed a tremendous popular and critical success here and in wartime England. Sturges was noticed as a decidedly new variation himself: a director who wrote his own pictures--movies that struck a contemporary comic nerve, rooted in satire as well as sentimentalism, and with an overriding intelligence monitoring the fun. After directing Christmas in July, Paramount, flabbergasted, noticed that Sturges had been working without a contract and finally gave him one. He never missed it. He made a deal with them that he expected to honor; he had learned early on from Solomon, his model of integrity, that a person is no better than his word.

Sturges drew on an inexhaustible energy while making his first films, an energy attributable in part to the remarkable influence of a book by Marie Beynon Ray titled How Never to Be Tired, or Two Lifetimes in One. He read her book while making McGinty and recognized the validity of her premise, namely, that fatigue is actually self-induced. The physical evidence of true fatigue dissipates in fifteen minutes. Thereafter, he gave the book to every friend and colleague who remarked that he was tired. "You'll get plenty of rest in the graveyard," Sturges reminded them. [60]

Apart from Sturges' movies were his inventions promoted through his engineering company, and his restaurant,

Preston Sturges on the "exercycle," one of his inventions, during the filming of <u>Christmas in July</u>, 1940.

The Players. In the summer of 1940, Sturges moved the equipment from "Snyders," a restaurant he had opened for Ted Snyder. "I had run it at a loss for two years. I purchased the site [for a new restaurant]. This for the purpose of using up my equipment," he noted.[61] The result was The Players Restaurant and Drive-In which opened for business in July 1940. A year later, it closed, then reopened soon after as a twenty-four-hour-a-day restaurant with Alexis Pillet, former headwaiter at The Ritz in New York and, later, proprietor of Pirolle's, as its manager. The Players provided Sturges with another opportunity to invent; and when he reopened it, tables now slid on tracks, windows automatically opened with the touch of a button, and a revolving bandstand held two orchestras, one to replace the other with no interruption in the music. And not the least of these inventions were a garbage hoist and a method of extricating undesirable customers by having tables lift from booths.[62]

The Players also became, like Michael Romanoff's restaurant and lounge, a popular meeting place for the Hollywood film community; and Sturges luxuriated in the role of host to a number of emigré film artists from occupied Europe, offering a congenial haven for Fritz Lang, Max Ophüls, René Clair, Jean Renoir, Julien Duvivier, Billy Wilder, and others. His hospitality became legendary and limitless, and tabs were run up only to be graciously and trivially forgotten by him.

The Great McGinty and Christmas in July created the confidence that provided Sturges with a latitude necessary to flower with his next project. The Lady Eve was the first big-budgeted film written and directed by him and cast with top stars, Henry Fonda and Barbara Stanwyck. Released in February 1941 to critical acclaim, it quickly became a box-office hit. The story of a female cardsharp contriving an elaborate scheme to season the gullible brewery heir she loves is one of the outstanding farces of the American screen. "It's perfectly wonderful," John Huston telegraphed Sturges, "and so are you."[63] Frank Lloyd Wright, fast becoming an ardent fan, began requesting private screenings of Sturges' films at his Taliesin Institutes in Scottsdale, Arizona, and Spring Green, Wisconsin. The Lady Eve was named the best film of the year by the New York Times and catapulted Sturges to the top as the major writer-director talent in Hollywood.

The Lady Eve was also Sturges' most complete synthe-

Orson Welles and Sturges dining at the latter's restaurant, The Players, in 1941. (The Museum of Modern Art/Film Stills Archive)

sis of dialogue and camera up to then, and an interesting argument for the stylistic choices he made in the editing and camera work. Albert Deane, director of foreign advertising and publicity at Paramount, questioned the aesthetic satisfaction of Sturges' editing technique in a letter to him. Sturges wrote an incisive reply:[64]

> When I got into the movies and began taking an interest in films I noticed that in some films I was conscious of the cutting and in some films I was not. And then I began to understand that there is a law of natural cutting and that this is what an audience in legitimate theatre does for itself. The more nearly the film cutter approaches this natural law of interest, the more invisible will be his cutting. If the camera moves from one person to another at the exact moment that you in the legitimate

theatre would have turned your head you will not be
conscious of a cut. If the camera misses by a
quarter of a second, you will get a jolt. (One
other requirement is necessary here: the two shots
must be approximately of the same tone value. If
you cut from white to black it is jarring.) To sum
it up, the camera must point at the exact spot the
audience wishes to look at any given moment. To
find that spot is absurdly easy: you have only to
remember where you were looking at the time the
scene was made. My friend Mamoulian told me he
could make the audience be interested in whatever
he showed them, and I told him he was mistaken.
It is true that he can bend my ear down and force
me to look at a doorknob when my reflex wants to
see the face of the girl saying goodbye, but it is
also true that it stops my comprehension of the
scene, destroys my interest and gives me a pain
in the neck.

The inscription on Sturges' screenplay of Sullivan's
Travels reads as follows: "This is the story of a man who
wanted to wash an elephant. The elephant darn near ruined
him."[65] Paramount bought his story for ten thousand dollars
and the entire production cost less than $680,000. With this
modest budget, Sturges made one of the most personal works
to come out of Hollywood. Blending comedy and melodrama
in a distinctively self-conscious fashion, Sullivan's Travels
is about a comedy film director who aspires to make serious
humanitarian works, only to learn after his exposure to an
unfair and cruel world that his comedy at least respected the
human spirit and palliated human suffering. The film appealed to the critics and the public, and Sturges delighted in
making it. "I have fun making movies," he said. "I never
write down to my audiences. I respect honest sentiment and
honest pratfalls."[66] This he did; and to prove the quantity
of laughs in this and subsequent pictures, he gauged his audiences' laughter with a laugh meter. In measurements of
laughter "force," Sturges counted one point for a chuckle,
two points for a laugh, three for a hearty laugh, and four
for a yell. The laugh meter yielded, for instance, at a
test screening at the Academy Theatre in Inglewood, California, on September 23, 1941: 131 ones, 54 twos, 23
threes, and 8 fours.[67]

Early in 1942, Sturges produced and wrote some of
René Clair's I Married a Witch, but took his name off as

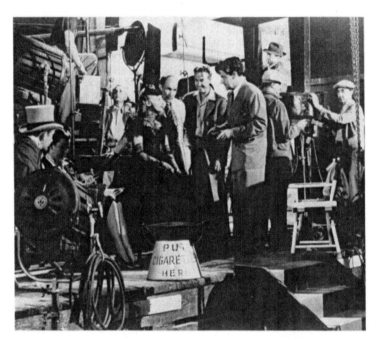

Sturges directs Veronica Lake in a scene from Sullivan's Travels. Cameraman John Seitz and editor Stuart Gilmore listen in. (The Museum of Modern Art/Film Stills Archive)

producer, contending that one cannot have a René Clair production by someone else. The hodgepodge of screenwriters included Dalton Trumbo, Marc Connelly, and Robert Pirosh. Trumbo felt useless on the project and eventually left, as did Sturges because of other commitments. His next film, The Palm Beach Story, was soon in production, with Sturges directing during the day portions of the script he had written the night before. A witty satire of the leisure class, remarkably written and acted, The Palm Beach Story was clearly another screen triumph for him. Released in November 1942, it did respectably well at the box office. Before the year was out, he had already written Triumph over Pain (The Great Moment), which encountered studio interference and was suspended from further production, and was involved in The Miracle of Morgan's Creek.

Sturges directing Eddie Bracken in <u>The Miracle of Morgan's</u>
<u>Creek</u>. (The Museum of Modern Art/Film Stills Archive)

No one could have expected that the story of a scatterbrained young woman who, in a convivial blur, marries an
unknown G. I., forgets the whole episode, and then finds herself pregnant, could ever have been produced in Hollywood at
the time. That the young woman, Trudy Kockenlocker, gives
birth to sextuplets makes it even more incredible. It has
been argued that the Hays Office let it pass probably because
no one quite understood exactly what happened. The production of Morgan's Creek was menaced with studio monitoring
and encountered censorship problems that kept it in limbo for
a brief period, but the issues were trivial ones. The preposterousness of Sturges' story line and the major thrust of
his satire remained astoundingly untouched. Perhaps because
of the censors' obtuseness, the wildness of Sturges' humor,
and his tenacity and enviable position at Paramount, Morgan's
Creek was perceived as less audacious and intellectual than
it is. Released in the first week of 1944 to extraordinary
praise, it was a box-office smash. The Miracle of Morgan's
Creek, simply put, represents the apex of Sturges' screenwriting and directing career and remains one of the landmark
social satires of sound film.

Sturges had been maintaining a mutually successful relationship with Paramount. Although he faced occasional studio
interference, the receipts on his films attested to the valuable
property he had become. He was, at this moment, the highest paid director on the Paramount lot. But this seemed not
enough. The editing problems he had been facing with Triumph over Pain, the biography--his only melodrama--of the
dentist William T. G. Morton, who discovered the anesthetic
benefits of ethyl chloride, were compounded with another new
problem on the production of his next film, Hail the Conquering Hero. Paramount executive producer Buddy DeSylva
didn't think Ella Raines was right for the romantic lead in
Sturges' story of a returning marine--Eddie Bracken--and
the glory lavished on him for his mistaken military valor.
Sturges, however, was adamant about retaining the actress
because, as he explained to DeSylva, she had already been
announced for the part and to pull her out at this stage could
ruin her new career. As far as the studio was concerned,
Sturges was in a financially advantageous position to be so
insistent, and DeSylva relented.

Hail the Conquering Hero almost equals the brilliance
of Morgan's Creek, and with a more complex expression of
sentimentalism and pathos that implicates any consummate
comedy. Hermine Isaacs saw it best in her review of the
film for Theatre Arts:[68]

One of the things that keeps Preston Sturges' work always new and refreshing is his skillful method of relating his most unregenerate comic hijinks frequently back to life. A scene of the lowest slapstick comedy, with no holds barred, will suddenly give way to a sober and sentimental scene with a touch so sure that no laugh lingers embarrassingly over from one moment to the next.

The nervous reaction to this kind of high-wire performance by a unique comedy stylist was also noticed by a fellow screenwriter. Dudley Nichols wrote to Sturges:[69]

> You are an original, you have done that amazing thing--created a new style, out of the best of the past in film plus 1000 units of Sturges Vitamins and a dash of pure courage. It's amazing how you keep the ball in the air all the time. I swore three times it was going to lob to the ground but each time you picked it up and sent it higher.

By mid-year of 1943, Sturges was indeed riding the crest. Respected by his colleagues and acclaimed by critics such as James Agee on the pages of The Nation, admirers such as Frank Lloyd Wright (who would write to him of Conquering Hero: "A remarkable portrait of America by America herself. Give us more--oh, much more of the sort."), and most every reviewer, his recognition was matched by tremendous returns at the box office.[70]

On June 9, 1944, two days after Conquering Hero was released, The Great Moment came out. Based on the book Triumph over Pain by René Fülöp-Miller, the film was originally to have been completed two years earlier. However, because of its strange innovative narrative, Paramount hesitated, then refused, to distribute it without significant changes. Stuart Gilmore was assigned to reedit it. The montage sequencing in The Great Moment was troublesome and anticlimactic for audiences. Also, in making it, Sturges had shown suffering and injury from war and this would not have made the picture popular with British audiences, who were fighting the war on their home front. Hence, the film's reediting.

Sturges objected to the streamlining of his picture and claimed that it made it much more incomprehensible. He also objected to its change of title from the original Triumph over Pain. (If the title had to be changed, he would have preferred one of his own suggestions-–Appointment with Destiny, One Against History, The Story of Blessed Slumber, or The Boston Tooth Yanker.) These were only two problems, however. The project was shelved as far back as early 1941, and contestations over the story of Morton had come in from university physicians, dentists, and Crawford W. Long's great-niece, asserting that others--Long, Horace Wells (not seen in a favorable light in Sturges' film), Charles Jackson--were the significant discoverers of early anesthesia. Fülöp-Miller's book came under attack for its inaccuracies. [71] Even the Joseph Burnett Company objected to the use of "Burnett's Bear Grease" in the publicity photographs as comedy relief at the expense of their pharmaceutical reputation. [72]

Sturges now reached the edge of his tolerance for the constant studio meddling he was encountering, and the time appeared right for a drastic change. The three-year contract he signed with Paramount expired on December 20, 1943, and Sturges chose not to renew it. At the end of the following month, he left the studio owing them one more film under the terms of his recently-expired contract. Paramount offered him an out by not paying him the thirty-thousand-dollar bonus they agreed to for each of the two films he was to direct. Sturges signed the agreement.

Sturges and Howard Hughes

Sturges left Paramount soon to engage in a truly ambitious venture at the beginning of 1944: to form a partnership with Howard Hughes, who wanted to invest in motion picture production. Sturges and Rupert Hughes, the novelist, playwright, and uncle of Howard, were friends, and Rupert brought Sturges and Hughes together. The lawyers of both parties attempted to negotiate a mutually satisfactory agreement, while Sturges and Hughes proceeded to form their own partnership. "On Saturday, February 12, 1944 during the afternoon," Sturges wrote, "Howard Hughes called me, said 'We have a deal?' After I explained why I said I might want to make an outside picture occasionally, we shook hands over the phone. "[73] California Pictures Corporation was formed. Sturges owned more than half of the capital voting stock and Hughes the rest under the title of the Hughes Tool Company. Still a third stock, non-voting shares, was bought $87\frac{1}{2}\%$ by Hughes and $12\frac{1}{2}\%$ by Henry Henigson, Sturges' old friend and a former producer at Universal and M-G-M during the 1930s. The union was certainly an uneasy alliance as far as the attorneys of both parties were concerned. Hughes was interested in putting in money and had an option to buy the principal shares after a ten-year period.

California Pictures started out offering Sturges the autonomy he wanted. It acquired his character, his habits. "We do a great deal of work around this office," he said. "My desk is full and disordered--I am allergic to normal efficiency. Here we are emotionally efficient."[74] Frank Moran, one of Sturges' stock company of actors at Paramount, with his gravel-voiced and tough demeanor, was a bright and well-read man and an old friend who visited between movie assignments. Some of Sturges' favorite pastimes included bowling and attending boxing matches, and Moran was a perfect companion, having fought Jack Johnson for the world heavyweight championship in Paris back in 1915 and Jess Willard in New York in 1916. Sturges was always providing conversation and thoughtfulness. What other film director would serve cocktails to his cast and crew every day after shooting? "He performed," one observer noted, "dozens of kindnesses for everyone."[75] He would come to the studio wearing one of his two berets, his trademark, and, as was his habit, worked twenty hours a day and slept four. Sturges gave up his pipe in favor of thirty to forty cigarettes a day and twenty cups of coffee. "That keeps me on edge," he said, "and I like it."[76]

Sturges enjoyed his independence, but it was an independence shadowed by the specter of Hughes's interest in California Pictures, the money he could put into it, and, consequently, the decisions he could make. As early as April of 1944, Sturges foresaw the situation that would develop, and he was concerned. He jotted it down in a random memo that expressed it succinctly:[77]

> In working for $2500 per week, or approximately $3500 per week less than I can command with the open market, I am investing $3500 a week in the venture which I hope to have returned through my % of the companies. If the board of directors has full say as to the companies' expenditures, how can I protect my investment?
>
> More and more my position looks like that of a salaried employee, a position I did not care to accept when Mr. Hughes first offered it to me.

A month later, the situation remained unmitigated. He wrote to Hughes:[78]

> My dear Howard,
>
> Upon reading the present edition of the various proposed contracts between us, it is apparent to me that it is going to take a long, long time to produce a document that both of us will be anxious to sign. In five months we have only just caught up with our first meeting in which you offered me a job as a salaried employee and I declined with thanks. A quick appraisal of the powers delegated to me in the present version of the contract will show you that I am still being offered the position of a salaried employee. To that proposition my answer remains the same.

On October 20, 1944, half of the board of directors--the screenwriter Jules Furthman; Sturges' agent, Frank Orsatti; and realtor Joseph De Bell--resigned.

At this time, Sturges was supervising the production of his screenplay of Prosper Mérimée's Colomba, retitled Vendetta, and hired Max Ophüls to direct it. Stuart Gilmore would edit. After a few weeks, a dissatisfied Hughes, for some eccentric personal reason, wanted Ophüls removed from the production and Sturges to take over. Hughes disliked Ophüls (ostensibly, he did not like foreigners), and the production was running over budget and behind schedule. And even though Sturges and Ophüls worked well together, Sturges had little choice but to acquiesce. The production of Vendetta was nonetheless subsequently postponed.

The initial production of California Pictures was Sturges' direction of his screenplay, The Sin of Harold Diddlebock, a comedy vehicle for and tribute to Harold Lloyd from an admirer. Harold Diddlebock started shooting on September 12, 1945, for two months, cost approximately $1,700,000 to make, and was released by United Artists on April 4, 1947. It was Lloyd's first picture since Professor Beware in 1938 and he did his own stuntwork for it.

The Sin of Harold Diddlebock, a reprise of Lloyd's belief in the pursuit of ambition, of making an idea a reality, was favorably received and did modestly well at the box office. In the story, Harold Diddlebock is fired from the same clerical job he had taken over twenty years earlier as a first step to success and fortune, and consequently finds a zany form of success in the incidental, accidental, purchase of a circus. William Du Bois chronicled the peculiarly accommodating relationship Sturges shared with Lloyd in his Sunday New York Times piece of March 17, 1946:[79]

> Lloyd originally planned to produce his own film, but when he decided instead to act in one, his only stipulation was that Sturges write and direct. It was also understood quite informally that any dispute over technique or story approach would be settled by a novel arbitration. Sturges would shoot the scene as he saw it, Lloyd likewise, and they would let the next morning's rushes decide the difference.

Harold Lloyd remarked in the same piece:

> 'Basically Preston and I think alike, even when our approach is different. I like to go on the set with a scene mapped out and work from my head; Preston comes on with a blueprint he's sweated over beforehand, to the last detail. He can do his cutting, a reel at a time, and stay with it indefinitely; it's an effort for me to sit in a projection room with an uncut story. After I've seen three good ideas go through the chopper, I have to come up for air.'

The slapstick in Harold Diddlebock, involving cliffhangers, high cranes, and a lion named Jackie, was inspired lunacy, and containing the chaos during the production was next to impossible. Louise Graf, the national representative of the public relations department of the American Red Cross, offered Sturges its facilities during the filming of the movie. "In times of peace," she wrote to him, "we aid in cases of disaster such as floods, fires, tornadoes, hurricanes, wrecks, etc.--assisting the civilians whenever necessary."[80]

The matter of Vendetta and Ophüls remained ill-resolved in Sturges' mind--and not forgotten. Hughes's growing participation in the production affairs from which he originally planned to steer clear now felt much like the studio interference Sturges had faced at Paramount. On October 30, 1946, Sturges resigned as an officer of California Pictures. Hughes, in accordance with his and Stur-

ges' agreement that either of them could end their professional
relationship at will, terminated their partnership. Soon after
its dissolution, Hughes had <u>Harold Diddlebock</u>, their one completed project together, shortened by approximately twenty
minutes and rereleased in 1950 through his own studio, R-K-O,
as <u>Mad Wednesday</u>.

Shortly before his resignation, Sturges received a letter from Vely Bey, from whom he hadn't heard in years.
Vely wrote from Brussels: ''I confess that I am quite surprised to discover that you are very well known here in Bel-
gium and what is more very favorably known--I always thought
you were very intelligent and that you would turn out to be
very bad or very good.''[81]   At the moment, it may have
seemed hard to recognize just how well he had turned out:
the inauspicious circumstances of leaving Hughes implied an
uncertain future.

<u>On the Ebb: The Not-So-Good Years</u>

Twentieth Century-Fox offered Sturges a contract to
work once again with them and, on December 11, 1946, he
signed to direct his screenplay of <u>Symphony Story</u> and another
film to star Betty Grable.   The U.S. Treasury Department
listed him as one of the country's highest-salaried residents
in 1947, which meant nothing since he had little ready cash.
He was involved in a lengthy, costly, and much-publicized
divorce suit from Louise and, by the middle of the year, The
Players became increasingly swamped with back debts.   Fox
was quickly beginning to appear as a necessary opportunity
toward--at least--financial stability.

Sturges wrote <u>Symphony Story</u> back in 1932 as a play.
A year later, he tried to have it filmed, but Samuel Marx
at M-G-M turned it down because it didn't fit into their production program.   Retitled <u>Unfaithfully Yours</u>, Fox was now
producing it, fifteen years later, at a cost of more than two
million dollars, one of their highest budgeted films to date,
with $300,000 of the total expenditure going to Sturges him-
self as his share of a one-film writer-producer-director deal.

Darryl Zanuck was enthusiastic about the film.   ''You
have written a magnificent script,'' he wrote to Sturges.[82]
The story of an egotistical maestro who fantasizes three

methods of dealing with his supposedly unfaithful wife, each
orchestrated to its appropriate composition, was a brilliant
idea. Rex Harrison, slated to play Sir Alfred De Carter,
cabled Zanuck from New York that he was thrilled at the
opportunity to work with Sturges.[83] And when Sturges encouraged suggestions for improving any of the details of the
script, Harrison exclaimed, "If anyone improves a line of
mine, I'll shoot him. It's a part better than Hamlet."[84]
Linda Darnell, playing Lady De Carter, was elated too. Seymour Stern noted in the Sunday New York Times of July 11,
1948: "She herself frankly states that throughout the production she felt as if she were moving in a dream. 'At last,'
she has said, again and again, 'I have found a director.'"[85]

Unfaithfully Yours indeed augured a return engagement
for Sturges, the farceur-director. But the production was
taking a long time--too long as far as Zanuck was concerned.
The movie was shot too grey, he thought, and looked muddy
and dirty. It should reek with brilliance. Even Fox's president, Spyros Skouras, interfered when he wrote a confidential
memo to Zanuck that the fantasy sequences might be confusing
to the average moviegoer, to which an irritated Zanuck replied:[86]

> Dear Spyros:
>
> If you had Shakespeare, Alexandre Dumas, and
> Ernest Hemingway combined they could not write a
> foreword that would in any fashion help the dream
> sequences as you cannot cure a subnormal intelli-
> gence level of certain audiences with subtitles.
> Anybody with a fourth grade education can under-
> stand what Harrison is trying to do and I think if
> we have to aim at those few imbeciles with a lower
> IQ rating we should go out of business. Unfaith-
> fully Yours according to all indications may not be
> a popular boxoffice [sic] picture but you cannot have
> it with last minute titles. Regards.
>
> Darryl

Zanuck did think, however, that the film was about
twenty minutes too long and that Unfaithfully Yours had abusive
production leniencies that allowed it to go a week over schedule. Eager to keep costs down, he cited it as an example of
what the studio must not tolerate in its future productions.
Unfaithfully Yours, an original and ambitious work, was

released in October 1948, made the studio little money, and the genius in its conception went sadly unrecognized by many of the critics.

Zanuck was eager to maintain Betty Grable's box-office appeal after the war and now wanted Sturges to concentrate exclusively on the western comedy he felt certain would be a successful vehicle for her. The Beautiful Blonde from Bashful Bend, adapted from a story by Earl Felton, is Sturges' only color film. His script for the movie bears little resemblance to its original source, but Felton was nonetheless delighted with it and didn't mind having his name connected with the production. 87 Sturges, though, was not enthused about the prospect of doing Beautiful Blonde; it was not his kind of film. He wrote to Zanuck back in late August of 1947 expressing his dissatisfaction:88

> ... I would be completely remiss in my job as producer if I failed to tell you that it would be very much wiser and better for all concerned to let me get to work immediately on a script of my own type which does not depend quite so much on jokes and luscious color for its acceptance.
> ... One such is my Symphony story [sic] that Ernst Lubitsch can tell you about. Boyer has always liked it and could probably be persuaded to play in it, possibly opposite Miss Grable. I have always refused to sell this story as I wanted to save it for my own company, but since you have already paid me a great deal of money and I feel a great emergency exists, I would be willing to part with it....
> [Preproduction work for Beautiful Blonde preceded the production of the "symphony story," which was, of course, to be Unfaithfully Yours. --Author]

Beautiful Blonde was shot from the end of September into the first week of December 1948. It went way over schedule, Zanuck meddled fiercely during the shooting, and matters became increasingly tense between director and production head. When The Beautiful Blonde from Bashful Bend was released on May 31, 1949, it was apparent that it would do little for the careers of anyone involved, especially for Sturges'.

After Beautiful Blonde, Zanuck lost faith in Sturges as a moneymaking director. Sturges and Twentieth Century-

Fox parted company on very unfriendly terms, and he found himself to be a "bad risk" in Hollywood thereafter. "When I found myself asking not how did I like a shot but how would Mr. Zanuck like it," Sturges remarked a few years later, "I knew I had had it in Hollywood."[89]

No Last Laugh

With no studio affiliation, Sturges spent much of 1949 writing screenplays. His first, Nothing Doing, or Mr. Big in Littleville, was purchased by M-G-M, and after he made the requested revisions, they decided not to produce it. During the following year, Sturges remained unemployed but worked on another screenplay, A Present for Uncle Popo, and wrote the book for the musical Make a Wish, based on his screenplay of The Good Fairy, which opened in New York at the Winter Garden in 1951.

In 1952, Sturges worked on Matrix, an old screenplay about a woman's relationship with two men she loves, one her husband, and how the consequences of her love for both result in his eventual suicide. Sturges carried Matrix with him throughout his movie career. He wrote it as a story back in the early 1930s and tried then to have Fox film it, but they claimed it was "too tragic."[90] He tried again in 1940 with Paramount and met with no success. Then he offered it to Zanuck, at Fox again, but Zanuck was unenthusiastic about it. Fox bought it anyway in December 1946 for fifty thousand dollars, then made a deal with Sturges to switch it for Symphony Story.

Early in 1952, Sturges finished a screen adaptation for Paramount on the Hugh Martin-Robert E. Lee Broadway musical, Look Ma, I'm Dancin'. The story, as he conceived it, was about a girl who studies ballet by mail and, armed with her diploma, goes to New York to make a career for herself. It was bought for Betty Hutton, but when she insisted that the film be directed by her new husband, a choreographer, the project was dropped. During this time, he also wrote a version of Roman Holiday for William Wyler, which Wyler didn't use; Sturges then offered notes and suggestions for the screenplay version he did use.

All of the artistic and financial setbacks during these first two years after leaving Fox were costing Sturges. In

April 1951, he added a dinner theatre and dance floor to his
restaurant to increase business, as the restaurant's con-
sistent losses were no longer a tax write-off against Sturges' filmmaking income. The dinner theatre, he thought,
would galvanize The Players to a novel status: a profit-
making entity that would also provide him with the opportunity to do some stage work of his own. He put on theatrical performances at The Players that included, among other
one-acters, Chekhov's The Bear; then a production of Room
Service with Eddie Bracken and Al Bridge; and, later, an
adaptation of Robert Sherwood's The Road to Rome. Many
from his old movie stock company performed in his productions
there. Stan Laurel, too, suggested a one-act farce, The
Dear Departed, to do.

One of the performers in The Players' productions
was a young woman named Anne--Sandy--Nagle, many years
Sturges' junior. They married in August 1951 and she would
give him two more sons, young Preston in February 1953
and Thomas, born in June 1956. Their age difference, en-
hanced by Sandy's childlike appearance, was so pronounced
that Sturges noted if this marriage didn't work, he could certainly turn around and adopt her. By early 1953, however,
the renovations on The Players nearly bankrupted them and,
soon after, both the Sturges Engineering Company and The
Players had to close.

Much of the next two years continued the pattern emerging in Sturges life: the constant optimism about projects
that, alas, would never materialize. In April 1953, he wrote
to George Templeton of a story idea titled The Great Hugo,
about "the last royal family in Europe with a king as chief
protagonist."91 Sturges was very excited about it and thought
it was one of the best film yarns he had ever come up with.
Nothing came of it. In August 1953, he left for New York to
direct his doctoring of a musical adaptation of Jacques Fey-
der's film, La Kermesse Héroïque (Carnival in Flanders),
with music by Jimmy Van Heusen, at the New Century Theatre. While in New York, Sturges signed a contract with
Lester Cowan to write and direct his own adaptation of Shaw's
The Millionairess. Katharine Hepburn had just finished the
London and New York stage runs of the play and was convinced it would make a marvelous film.

In January 1954, Sturges and his family sailed for
London to shoot the movie. There, too, other possibilities
for continental film work might arise. The stalled funding

for the production of The Millionairess kept it postponed until Hepburn had to leave England to honor prior commitments. Another property he was trying to have produced there, however, was his screenplay about a king who takes out insurance against his title. Long Live the King, which was to star Michael Redgrave, was an emerging reality for him during most of 1956, but it, too, finally ran into money problems.

Sturges' only completed film project after he left America was suggested by a series of satirical columns in Le Figaro by Pierre Daninos on the foibles of the French as seen through the eyes of an Englishman. The Notebooks of Major Thompson was shot concurrently in French and English and was successful in Europe. Sturges was hired by Gaumont in 1954 to write a screenplay using the title "Les Carnets du Major Thompson" and was working on his own original screenplay when Daninos' columns were collected in a book that became a national bestseller in France. Gaumont, fearful of disappointed audiences, asked Sturges to write another screenplay incorporating the Daninos articles.

Sturges' intention was to film a sequential work that attempted to transfer, or translate, the essay form of the original series into a movie. However, despite Gaumont's requirement, something went wrong, clearly wrong. It was, the critic Penelope Houston wrote in 1965, "as though somewhere along the line the mainspring of that perfect comedy timing had snapped."[92] There are moments of genuine funniness, but too few, and the voice-over narration fails to integrate them into a personal representation of character and situation, an integration for which Sturges had become great. Jack Buchanan acclaimed him as "the smoothest director I've worked with since Lubitsch."[93] But the genius unfortunately appeared battle-weary and exhausted. The Notebooks of Major Thompson was released in the United States on May 21, 1957, under the title The French They Are a Funny Race, to generally unfavorable reviews and no financial success.

In February 1957, The Great McGinty was being considered as a musical for the Broadway stage with E. Y. Harburg doing the score and with a later plan for Paramount to film it. Norman Panama and Melvin Frank would write and direct it. Sturges was outraged that someone else would handle his work when he was readily available, and wrote to Y. F. Freeman, a vice-president at Paramount:[94]

> I have always wondered why the movie industry was
> so firmly persuaded that the original author could
> be of no possible help in the case of a remake or
> any other change in a work. I always felt, on the
> contrary, that the man who was adroit enough to
> make it a hit in the beginning would be the man
> most apt to be helpful the second or third time
> around. Past performance means as much in the
> realm of men as it does in horsedom.

MCA wanted twenty-five thousand dollars and a third of the
movie sale for a two-year option. The deal was never made.

Throughout the rest of 1957, Sturges was absorbed
with his play, J'appartiens à Zozo (I Belong to Zozo), originally written in French the previous year. Zozo takes place
in the penthouse of the son of "the only Russo-Greco-Balko-
Albanian family that ever got out of its country with its fortune intact."[95] Zozo's mother, Madame Zazzaroff, owns the
biggest hotel in Paris and his penthouse is on top of it.
Practically all of the hotel's employees are cousins. Sturges was eager to stage it in Paris first, but Zozo could not
find a producer, so he gave a synopsis to Herman Shumlin,
who, in turn, passed it on to Max Gordon. Gordon wasn't
interested; he thought Zozo was "a little too wild for him."
Sturges replied from Paris:[96]

> Zozo is actually one of the funniest ideas I've ever
> had ... worked out in a comedy technique I de-
> veloped during twenty years in Hollywood ... a
> technique, incidentally, that always scared the be-
> jeesus out of producers, but that occasionally
> amused the public. My dearest friends and sever-
> est critics constantly urged me to cut the pratfalls
> down from five to three, but actually it was the
> enormous risks I took ... in skating right up to
> the edge of non-acceptance [sic] ... that paid off
> so handsomely. There are certain things that will
> convulse an audience ... when it is already soft-
> ened up by what has occurred previously ... that
> seem very unfunny in cold print.

Gordon then decided to read the entire English version of the
play, but his feelings remained unchanged. Sturges ran into
Katina Paxinou, who, after doing a glut of classical tragedies,
accepted the role of Madame Zazzaroff if Zozo were to be
staged. But while Sturges was trying to find a producer for

it, other more financially expedient possibilities distracted him from continuing his search--possibilities that, like J'appartiens à Zozo, never materialized.

The end of 1957 and all of 1958 held the promise of only more silenced efforts. Sturges considered The Gentleman from Chicago, a comic screenplay about the problems befalling a deported gangster, among his best story ideas, and a French company signed a deal to purchase the screenplay for Sturges to direct. "Can anything go wrong?" a wary Sturges asked. He was assured the deal was set.[97] A month later, word got around that Stanley Donen was working on a similar picture about a Chicago gangster (Surprise Package), and although the Sturges and Donen stories were completely different, the French company pulled out. In November of 1957, Sturges proposed a remake of The Power and the Glory to Fox, but Skouras thought it wouldn't sell. The Metamorphosis of Philip Musica, a screenplay draft based on Robert Shaplen's New Yorker stories about the Wall Street swindler F. Donald Coster, was a picture possibility that also fell through at the end of the year. By the middle of 1958, Sturges was working on the final draft of a French translation of Robert Sherwood's historical comedy of Hannibal, The Road to Rome. Back in America a short while now, he was always preoccupied with new projects or attending to old ones. "I have gotten over the Great Hollywood Disease," he said, "the inability to think when you're off salary about anything but 'Where am I going to get that $6000 a week?'"[98]

Still, there was too little money. Sandy and their small sons returned to California but planned to join him soon in New York where Sturges was proposing a television series to NBC called It Happened Exactly Here, an anthology of weekly dramatic shows, each centered on an historical site. Sturges was intrigued by the possibilities of television but saw the insurmountability of its situation. "I said I was a fast writer," he said, "but I couldn't do seventeen Miracle of Morgan's Creeks in a year."[99] He also proposed two other ideas: Plays I Always Wanted to See Again, which involved interviewing famous theatre personalities about their favorite stage work and then showing a piece of it televised afterward, and Station F. A. T. E. about just that--how fate determines the course of people's lives. None was ever realized.

On August 6, 1959, Preston Sturges died of a heart attack in his office at the Algonquin Hotel in New York, where he was working on his autobiography, The Events Leading Up to My Death, for Henry Holt. He started it years earlier in Hollywood and now was in the process of completing it.

No tribute can truly commemorate a life lived with adventure and distinguished by the integrity of fairmindedness and hard work. But the vision and comic genius of Preston Sturges at his best is the earned product of such a life and of the writer's and director's art. "I have never done anything but my very best work for anyone, and to do this and retain my first fine enthusiasm over a period of thirty years has required a rather special set of working conditions," he wrote to Howard Hawks in 1956. [100]

> Like Carnation's Contented Cows, I have been a happy writer, and this happiness came from hope.... I have always insisted upon good odds, and whether I was gambling for fame or money or a stake in a new picture company, I have always had flops like everybody else, but never because I thought my second best was good enough for what I was getting. I think it was this very atmosphere which caused me to do pretty good work as much as any native ability I might have inherited.

For Mary Dempsey's son, it is a fair and honest assessment, and an honorable one.

2

THE SCREENWRITING OF PRESTON STURGES

> Jimmy: You know, you're not like other girls.
> Tulip (softly): No?
> Jimmy: No. There's a sort of sour quality about
> you that's refreshing.
> Tulip: Do I thank you or slap your face?
> Jimmy: You know what I mean. You're sort of
> like lemonade. Instead of being sweet and sticky
> like cream soda ...
> Tulip: You have a wonderful choice of words,
> haven't you?
> Jimmy (taking her seriously): I have facility of
> expression.
> Tulip: What?
> Jimmy: Honest I have. I know it sounds sort of
> swellheaded, but I can use words and some day
> if I get the chance you'll see if I can't.
>
> --from The Crepe Hanger (a 1931 version of
> Christmas in July)[1]

The touchstone of Preston Sturges' screenwriting art lies in the respect paid to the play and density of verbal language. The criteria for judging the success of most any Sturges screenplay invariably include the standard of eloquence found in the twist of a phrase, a phonic rhythm, a defiant quickness, and, often, a speed that characterizes the seeming effortlessness of "talk." Manny Farber once wrote that this talk turned Sturges' pictures "into a kind of open forum where everyone down to the cross-eyed bit player gets a chance to try out his oratorical ability."[2] This general perception of Sturgesian language is quite right. However, the privilege of this chance comprises only part, albeit the most significant part, of Sturges' screenwriting. And writing of this kind,

55

tonic and perfidiously adventuresome, establishes the standard
of eloquence as one of poetry, of a cacophony of Euro-
American vernacularisms and utterances, peculiarly--and ap-
propriately--spoken with scandalous indifference.

The remarkable quality of this "wacky dream language
drawing equally on the energy of the new world and the subtlety of the old"3 reverses our expectations of character roles
in narrative cinema. Here Sturges creates a distinction between character types and what they are traditionally obliged
to say. A William Demarest, a Jimmy Conlin, an Al Bridge,
or a Frank Moran mystify the function of the supporting and
bit player with a spectacular pronouncement of attitude and an
overlay of sensibility that reestablish the conventional dramatic
roles of these characters while recognizing the apparatus of
sound film in furnishing their "talk" with speed, pacing, and
buoyancy.

The kinetic impact of language presented through this
style brings us to the second standard of Sturges' screenwriting, particularly for his comedies: the speed and dynamic
of spoken language become the crucial rhythmic pattern (or
patter) that creates the frenzy and provokes the tentative acts
and involuntary reflexes that his characters display, both in
language and image. Indeed, at this point our concern does
shift to the image of characters; for in his characters'
speech, Sturges incarnates a spirit of determined individual-
ism, of energy anthropomorphized in the pursuit of accomplishing a semblance of order in the world and in the process
hoping to net a respectable share of personal success. The
expectations vary: for Luisa, in Sturges' 1934 screenplay of
Ferenc Molnár's play, The Good Fairy, it is literally to be
the "good fairy," to do always good deeds; for McGinty and
Sullivan, it is the desire to do good for society; for Jean and
Norval, it is the conquest of romance; and for Woodrow Truesmith, it is nothing less than the wish to be seen in the pure
light of truth.

The last inflection of the last line in the scripts unal-
terably written by Preston Sturges presents us with characters
woven into personal narratives. "All my actors wear tailor-
made parts, down to the woman who sells flowers on the
street," Sturges said. "What you see on the screen is the
work of one man; what you hear is his voice. Like it or
not, you know exactly whom to praise--or blame."4 The
density and sophistication of verbal play that define his characters is the starting point for any discussion of Sturges'

screenwriting art. For here is the essential form, crafted according to the conventions of dramatic structure and film-making style. The perception of language at Sturges' most powerful spins his whole narrative into orbit, and this sense of speed amounts to nothing short of conquering the medium with an indelible vision of the world on the verge of cata-clysm. "As the words sluice out of the actors' mouths," Manny Farber noted, "the impression is that they teeter on the edge of a social, economic, or psychological cliff and that they are under some wild compulsion to set the record straight before plunging out of the picture."5

Sturges' earliest screenwriting was part of a collab-orative effort with other scenarists and dialogue writers that invites speculation about his original contribution to these projects. Instead of culling through this early filmography--from 1930 to the time of The Power and the Glory in 1933--the emphasis on the kind of screenwriting Sturges did that signaled the versatility to be found in his later work appears primarily in four screenplays: The Power and the Glory, The Good Fairy, Easy Living (1937), and, most completely, in Remember the Night (1939). Diamond Jim (1935) and his adaptation of Justin Huntly McCarthy's historical drama about François Villon, If I Were King (1938), are properties with thematic tie-ins to other work. Diamond Jim shows us a protagonist whose power and influence follow Tom Garner's and certainly antecede McGinty's, five years later. And the poet-criminal Villon suggests the same passionate spirit Stur-ges tried to infuse in his character of the pioneer inventor William Morton. However, the models of screenwriting that best display the ambiguous point of view, creative use of flashback, density of verbal comedy and complexity of comic structure, and a poignant melodrama--all evident in Sturges' later work--are the aforementioned four.

With The Power and the Glory, Sturges acquired the distinction of being the sole writer of his movie. This first screenplay completely written by him not only established well-known precedents about the role of the screenwriter (see profile section), but, oddly, was a somber melodrama written in, what was considered at the time, a sophisticated and technical narrative style. Here, comedy could not be further removed in presenting this story of a man's rise to power and the complications it creates in his character. Spencer Tracy's Tom Garner does indeed prefigure Orson Welles's Kane in his success, as has often been suggested. Not in

Director William K. Howard, screenwriter Preston Sturges, and producer Jesse L. Lasky at Fox Studios during the making of The Power and the Glory, 1933. (The Museum of Modern Art/Film Stills Archive)

a drive for success, as we see later in Jim Brady, and even
to some extent in McGinty, but in the manipulation of great
power and influence and the melancholy nature behind the now
effortless exercise of it. The choices of action leave Tom
Garner unhappy, especially when he feels the heavy price of
power in his alienation from others and his family and in the
diminishment of the personal happiness that is so much a
promised part of this success.

Sturges structured his story by using a flashback "narratage" technique of punctuating the story action with a nar-
rated commentary intended to render an oblique point of view.
We see the episodes in Tom's life that chronicle his rise to
power, but, finally, do not explain the mystery of his character and brooding. Like Kane, Garner perplexes us with
an ambiguity inspired by the complexity of living through the
events of one's life. And in the sequential reordering of
these episodes--a technique used nine years later with the
life of William Morton in The Great Moment--Sturges re-
fracted the narrative to distort our perception of time so
that we may respond more consciously to its value (a technical aim much like that of the nouveau roman in literature).

The flashback technique in the script combines words
and images in a duality of purpose. Throughout the film,
Henry and his wife offer different profiles of Tom Garner:
a man destined for greatness or one who is simply ruthless,
a betrayed family man or a neglectful husband and father, a
conscientious business leader or a callous tycoon. All of
these impressions are softened by the noncommittal image
of Spencer Tracy's Garner, posed, finally, as neither hero
nor tyrant. Hence, the project of placing judgment on human
actions, necessary as it may be, is finally of moot value.
As Andrew Sarris noted: "Throughout his career, Sturges
employed the flashback not so much to express the selfish
subjectivity of memory, but to reorganize, restructure, and
resequence reality so that all its ironies, comic and tragic,
can be more effectively expressed."6 This use augurs the
related distance and unsentimentality of Sturges' coolest and
most ironic screenplays: The Great McGinty, Unfaithfully
Yours and, to some extent, The Miracle of Morgan's Creek.
The flashback is not the dominant device written into these
screenplays, but the tonicity produced through it in The Power
and the Glory is certainly resonant in these later works.

In contrast to The Power and the Glory and Diamond

Jim, his grim portraits of the enigmatic powerful, Sturges
adapted a delightful play in 1934 that illustrates well the verbal comedy for which we would come to know him best. The
screenplay for The Good Fairy, based on Ferenc Molnár's
play, is gentler, more playful and innocent in its comedy,
and less satirical than Molnár's play. Sturges displays the
possibilities of a density of dialogue much more in his screenplay of an innocent girl who earnestly tries to do a good deed
every day. Luisa is surely the "good fairy" in virtue and
benevolence. And here her innocence is compromised, not
to grim consequences, but to a final celebration of romance.
The play, and the screenplay, evoke the storybook quality of
a Central European romance where so many classical comedy
conventions, once unraveled, promise the suitably matched
couples a lifetime of happiness.

Molnár, alas, lacks Schnitzler's vision and critical
perception of society, but Sturges clearly has the facility to
be something like both at once--captivating with his marvelous characters and language yet mildly satiric of their
foibles. However, The Good Fairy makes most of its con-
cessions to the storybook tale and reveals through them Sturges' mastery in writing scenes of mistaken identities and
motives (Luisa's encounter with Konrad at supper in his suite
and her first meetings with Dr. Sporum) and of utter verbal
delight. Here, and in his incomplete screenplay written for
M-G-M in 1936 and based on another, later, Molnár play,
Great Love, Sturges finds the perfect format of situation
comedy through which to practice this verbal playfulness.
For instance, Molnár wrote the following passage in the first
act of this play:[7]

> Her Excellency: All right, then. Now let me hear
> who this Louis person is for whom I put up such
> a heroic fight. (Makes herself comfortable)
> Margit: The Louis person, Your Excellency, I
> mean Louis Csok, has been engaged to Irene for
> the last four years. He is an engineer, as I
> told you before. We are very proud of him.
> He has two great inventions: one is a device
> to hold rails in place, and the other is a peat
> burning furnace. But he excels not only as a
> technician--but as a man--he is the fencing
> champion.
> Her Excellency: Marvelous!
> Margit: He won second prize at the Olympic games.
> Her Excellency: Stupendous!

> Margit: He is an exceedingly good, decent fellow.
> Our poor mother really selected him for Irene.
> He is a sort of distant relative of ours. Mother
> was born an Emoed. The son of her brother,
> Emmerich Emoed, married a Shukorszky girl,
> Anna Shukorszky. Anna's sister, Hermine Koro,
> née Shukorszky, divorced Steven Koro and mar-
> ried Elmer Csok, who had three brothers: An-
> drew, Paul and Alexander ...

But Sturges transformed it into a scene distinctively his own.
Complete with funny names, predisposed confusions, and plain
wackiness, Margit attempts to explain her younger sister's
amorous relationship with Louis Csok ("C̲sok like Kazoo") to
the Baron:[8]

> Margit: Louis was practically a relative. You see
> Mother was born an Emu. The son of her broth-
> er, my uncle Emmerich Emu, married a Shukor-
> sky girl, Anna Shukorsky. Anna's sister, Her-
> mine Koro, born Shukorsky, of course, divorced
> Stephen Koro and married Ferenc Csok.
> Baron: I don't blame her.
> Margit: Ferenc had three brothers: Mathew ...
> Baron (nodding): Mark, Luke and Paul.
> Margit (smiling perfunctorily): T̲h̲r̲e̲e̲, your Excel-
> lency. Mathew, Paul and Alexander ...

This passage also illustrates Sturges' "hook" system,
a popular device used time and again in his screenwriting to
sustain Sturgesian talk. Sturges' biggest problem in writing
his first stage play, The Guinea Pig, was in bringing his
characters' conversations to such a complete end that little
was left to be said. Conversations and ideas were so fully
developed that nothing remained for the next character to
hook on to. He solved this by inventing his hook system
whereby a hook exists as a word, key thought, or motif that
allows another character to carry on, to amplify, or to
pivot--in a totally different direction--the dialogue or idea at
hand. The hook system sustains a running dialogue so well
that "the problem," noted Alva Johnston in his 1941 Saturday
Review piece on Sturges, "becomes that of making the dialogue
end instead of that of keeping it going."[9] A more sophisticated example of the hook system appears a few years later
in the screenplay for Hail the Conquering Hero. In this
scene, Woodrow, having confessed his hoax and expecting
public excoriation, is surprised to find that the townspeople

still support him for mayor. Sturges explains this attitude
through veterinarian Doc Bissell:[10]

> Doc Bissell: Politics is a very peculiar thing,
> Woodrow ... if they want you, they want you
> ... they don't need reasons any more ... they
> find their own reasons ... just like when a
> girl wants a man ...
> Libby: That's right ... you don't need reasons,
> although they're probably there.

From this disturbing idea that we may, perhaps unconscion-
ably, justify most any public action we choose, Sturges pivots
the explanation to reaffirm Libby's love for Woodrow. Furthermore, just as Libby's love comes not without merit, without "reasons," so Sturges implies that there are sound reasons for the townspeople's perception of Woodrow as a decent
character. (This moment in the film follows a frightening
scene of a mob of residents emerging toward Woodrow. The
ambivalent tone of this entire sequence, disquieting and never
fully placated, is brought up later.)

Sturges' freewheeling delight in punctuating many of his
screenplays with moments that bear no connection to the linear development of the story appears in The Good Fairy, as
it does in Easy Living, Sullivan's Travels, and The Sin of
Harold Diddlebock. When Dr. Sporum buys the latest model
pencil sharpener with his newly found subsidy, the attention
lavished on this minor marvel is quintessential Sturges. "It
must have bearings! Glorious! Like a needle! Feel it!
Did you ever see such a point?" gasps Sporum. Such hitherto undisclosed awe from him feeds a comic bit and shows a
perception of peccadillo mined of its humorous effect and for
which Sturges never hesitated to stop the whole show to ac-
centuate. Earlier in the story, Luisa, no longer under the
guardianship of the orphange, takes a job in town as a movie
usher. To avoid a confrontation with Detlaff, she escapes
into the audience and watches the movie, an early sound film.
The scene following is pure Sturges and not in Molnár's play.
Sturges gives equal attention to Luisa's innocence and sympathy for the romance on the screen and to the triteness of
the movie, here, within our movie. And the latter, mocked
to perfection as a relic of the archaic technology of the earliest talkies, shows how effortlessly Sturges could write this
scene. Here he has Luisa engrossed in this silly melodrama
as the movie's romantic lead stoically refuses his lover's
return. His replies reduced but to a simple command, he

tells her to "go," not once but repeatedly:[11]

> Mitzi: Meredith! Meredith! Ooooh!
> Meredith: Go.
> Mitzi: Oh, Meredith! Meredith! If you only ...
> give me a chance to explain!
> Meredith: Go.
> Mitzi: Go?
> Meredith: Go.
> Mitzi: Oh, but Meredith! Ah!
> Meredith: Go!
> Mitzi: You don't mean that, Meredith!
> Meredith: Go!
> Mitzi: Oh, Meredith! (Sobs) Surely you don't
> understand me!
> Meredith: Go!

All the while in the scene, Meredith stands stationary at a spot from which he dares not move for fear of being too far away from the microphone.

Many moments such as these constitute the substance of Sturges' dialogue writing and scene structuring. But cataloguing them serves a small end in accounting for the attitudes and tone evident throughout entire sequences in the films written by Sturges, and certainly throughout nearly all of the films written and directed by him. The two works that evince the guiding spirit of Preston Sturges during this period, distinctively and authoritatively, are Easy Living and Remember the Night. The Power and the Glory and Diamond Jim exhibit Sturges' fascination with power in America, but their portentously tragic tone never suggests the other side of Sturges. If their lineage was to include The Great McGinty and The Great Moment, Easy Living and Remember the Night are the parallel lineage from which The Lady Eve, The Palm Beach Story, The Miracle of Morgan's Creek, Hail the Conquering Hero, and The Sin of Harold Diddlebock will come. Sullivan's Travels may be seen as a hybrid of the two.

Easy Living and Remember the Night present Sturges' screenwriting art at its pinnacle prior to McGinty. Mitchell Leisen directed both films, but their dominant features are clearly the charm of the players and Sturges' scripts. Easy Living extends further than before the congestion and fast pace of comic dialogue and the inextricable relationship between mania and dialogue. In Easy Living, the first justification for Sturgesian storytelling occurs: there is no reason

for the story to be told, no comic or melodramatic resolution
to be met, other than the creation of complications for the
amusement of unraveling them.   Here, a sable coat is thrown
from a Fifth Avenue penthouse window and lands on Jean Arthur's head while she rides an open-air bus.   Astonished, she
looks around to the Hindu swami in back of her and cracks,
"What's the big idea, anyway?"   "Kismet," he replies.

This idea--kismet, fate, an arbitrary turn of the plot--
will shape almost every Sturges screenplay henceforth, either
in respect or defiance of generic traditions.   Edward Arnold,
Jean Arthur, Ray Milland, and Luis Alberni encounter a series of confusions, obstacles, and misapprehensions which
Sturges designed to fuel verbal exchanges ever more furiously
at each attempt to straighten them out.   Mary Smith (Arthur)
falls upon--more aptly, has fallen upon her--a fur coat which
leads to J.B. Ball (Arnold), which leads Louis Louis (Alberni) to suspect she is J.B.'s mistress, which leads Mrs. Ball
(Mary Nash) to believe Mary is J.B.'s lover, which leads to
his son's (Milland) encounter with her in his father's office.
He falls in love with her.   The truth of her identity is exposed.   The older couple is reunited and a new, younger
couple is united.

The links of this chain form a circle that, like the
classical comedy structure, does lead to a renewal and celebration.   But Sturges has also taken the conventions of comedy and turned them into an elaborate mix-up, as well as
stretching the idea of knowing to the nth degree in both directions.   Here we see Edward Arnold's J.B. in total dark-
ness and exasperated by the absurd behavior of those around
him.   And at the opposite end, Sturges invented that marvelous human redundancy, hotelier Louis Louis ("For everything you wish, we anticipate.   Even before you ask."   "Too
far is enough!").   From a character who knows nothing to a
character who knows twice, Sturges runs amok creating people who produce sublime confusion and a multiplicity of purposes.   In Easy Living, the achievement of these purposes
ostensibly structures the story, but it also does much more:
as an array of the misrepresented; Mary Smith, J.B. Ball,
Ball, Jr., and Louis Louis are conduits, in that peculiarly
theatrical yet quite artless style, for Sturgesian "talk."

To match his virtuosity in comedy screenwriting, Sturges wrote a poignant and remarkably sentimental movie in
1939, his last screenplay before The Great McGinty.   Re-

member the Night is not only the prototype for the finest kind
of Sturgesian melodrama, but sets the tone of sincerity and
innocence that would later characterize the most nakedly in-
genuous side of Sturges. Indeed, the integrity of Sturges'
vision, his emotional response to his art and culture, and
his deepest involvement with human feelings appear in the
striking juxtaposition of the very comic and the very touching.
This sometimes disrupted the tone of his films; but more often than not, the schism created a tension complex with emotional and intellectual ambivalences. As a product of his
writing, the ingenuousness of Sturges' melodramatic moments
verges on the maudlin, but never succumbs to it. The lilt
and rhythm of his best sequences has characters of intelligence and wit, of ordinarily sharp contours, offering gentle
admissions.

Here Fred MacMurray's prosecuting attorney confesses
his love for Barbara Stanwyck, the defendant, on their drive
back to New York after spending the Christmas holidays at
his mother's farm in Indiana. When Lee insists that she
doesn't love him, Sargent answers: "I suppose that's why
you've looked at me the way you have, and danced with me
the way you did and kissed me the way you did, and your
hand has always found mine and mine has always found yours
when they were anywhere near each other."[12]

The counterbalance to the gentleness in Remember the
Night is not the zaniness of screwball comedy, but the kind
of sarcastic wit found in Sturges' best mature work. The
sharpness of Lee Leander and John Sargent when we first
see and listen to them hardly prepares us for the sentimentalism later in the film. New York City at Christmastime
has its charm, as Leisen's camera shows us, but the slap-
in-the-face briskness of Lee and John's first encounters an-
chors this side of Sturges-the-wise-guy in a city of cheaters.
Here, in New York, in court and in the district attorney's
office, there are no illusions of future happiness nurtured by
the coziness of a small-town holiday interlude, only a jail
sentence for Lee. And when John takes custody of her for
the holidays, nothing stops Sturges from continuing to create
a totally honest and unsentimental character. Lee debunks
any explanation less than the truth for her stealing. Per-
spectives, she knows, far more than conventional reasons,
govern one's actions. She tells John in the following scene:[13]

      Sargent: Did you take things you didn't need?
      Lee: Sure.

Sargent: In the presence of beautiful things did you feel a sudden irresistible urge to take them with your hands and hurry away with them?

Lee (Faintly amused): You mean was I hypnotized?

Sargent (Hopefully): I mean maybe you're a kleptomaniac.

Lee (Placidly): No, they tried that. You see, to be a kleptomaniac you can't sell any of the stuff afterwards ... or you lose your amateur standing.

Sargent: I don't understand it. First you think it's environment and then ... then you think it's heredity ... and you get some bird with seven generations of clergymen behind him.

Lee: I don't think you ever could understand because your mind is different. Right or wrong is the same for everybody, you see, but the rights and wrongs aren't the same. Like in China they eat dogs.

She continues to explain to him:

Lee: Try it like this: suppose you were starving to death ...

Sargent: Yes.

Lee: ... and you didn't have any food and you didn't have any money and you didn't have any place to get anything.

Sargent: Yes.

Lee: And there were some loaves of bread out in front of a market, and you were starving to death and the man's back was turned ... would you swipe one?

Sargent (Vehemently): You bet I would!

Lee (Smiling with pleasure): That's because you're honest. You see, I'd have a six-course dinner at the table d'hote across the street and then say I'd forgotten my purse.

As Sargent looks at her goggle-eyed she concludes sweetly:

You get the difference?

Sargent: I think yours is smarter.

Lee's hardness undergoes a mellowing process after they leave the city and Sturges carries it out during the rest of the story until the end when they must return to trial. He creates a vivid portrait of small-town life that crosses from reality into a kind of fantasy through which Sturges reclaims an innocence not only of one's childhood, but of another, simpler and more loving, world than that to which Lee and John must inevitably return. Here, a spotless old house in the country, home baking, and the so-clean and fresh accommodations of a hospitable widowed mother and her sister provide the promise of safety and comfort. These characters, too, are not ignorant or unsophisticated; they have the intelligence of common sense and suggest that they know the world extends beyond the small scope of their lives. Yet they emerge as models of benevolence and serenity in their own world. Sturges wrote scenes of such breathtaking sweetness that one is left staggered by his facility to characterize so poignantly human warmth after the hardness of his opening sequence. Nothing ritualizes this small-town idyll more beautifully, for example, than the New Year's Eve barn dance Lee attends with John. In preparation, Mrs. Sargent (Beulah Bondi) alters an old-fashioned party dress for Lee that she used to wear when John's father was alive. She asks Lee if she loves John and tells her that John is in love with her. The scene later on when Lee appears in the dress is transforming: she has become a living vision of the past, stunningly reincarnated, as John gazes with wonder. Leisen's camera reveals the delicacy of this moment, but the preoccupation with innocence and its attendant sincerity has indeed been Sturges' and will continue to appear throughout his directorial career.

Several years earlier, Sturges wrote the first draft of a screenplay titled The Biography of a Bum and no one was much interested in producing it. As with other plays and screenplays--A Cup of Coffee (aka Christmas in July) and Symphony Story (aka Unfaithfully Yours)--he kept it aside and, when the opportunity arose in 1940, arranged to parlay his substantial writing salary for a chance to direct his own material. For a token fee of ten dollars, Sturges literally gave Paramount his screenplay on the condition that he make his own picture. This landmark decision not only paved the way for other filmmakers to write and direct their films, but gave Sturges all the resources of the medium to define further his vision of society and to explore the dimensions of comedy and melodrama.

The Great McGinty is a critical starting point because it so totally expresses the dark mood and pessimism of Preston Sturges that it is difficult to imagine the direction

A living vision of the past: Barbara Stanwyck and Fred MacMurray in Remember the Night. (The Museum of Modern Art/Film Stills Archive)

his future work would take. As a screenplay, The Great McGinty forsakes much of the funniness of Sturges' later screenplays for a sarcasm that bathes its laughs with an unredeemed despondency. McGinty shows us a vagrant with no political inclination defrauding the system with little effort to attain political power beyond anyone's expectation, only to lose it when he concedes to a humanitarian impulse that becomes, as Sturges shows it, the debility to a greater success in the world. McGinty will aid the poor and exploited and will learn that nothing effectual will come of it.

I have written elsewhere of the episodic structure of McGinty and the Brechtian kind of distance created by it. But this comes from the fusion of the script, editing, and camera, just as Brecht's epic drama finds its fuller expression in its staging. In his screenplay, however,

Sturges recreated another idiom, one peculiarly American
and indebted to the tradition of the political satire of car-
toonist Thomas Nast. McGinty, the Boss, and Catherine--
all acquire the black-white qualities that, despite the characters into which they develop, are typed according to the
virtues and evils they represent. McGinty and William Demarest as "the politician" truly are "mugs," as the Boss de-
scribes them; and he is himself a blackguard, corrupted to
the core and sometimes stupid. Catherine McGinty, on the
other hand, embodies an essential goodness that Sturges ex-
aggerates for his screenwriting purposes. Perhaps it is because the consequences of virtues such as decency and justice count so heavily on Sturges' ethical scorecard in McGinty that we shrink at a total justification of McGinty's wife.
There is a cynicism behind her function as the civilizing
force in his life. While Sturges sympathizes with her sense
of goodness, he presents it as the virtue of someone whose
innocence is a crippling liability in the real world. Nonetheless, there is a peculiar sense of judgment in Catherine
McGinty, not unlike Sturges' own perspective of fairness,
that mitigates her blindness. "What you rob you spend,
and what you spend goes right back to the people," she explains to William Demarest, "so where's the robbery?"[14]

But Sturges routs this logic with the contention that
nothing much ever changes, and his position is a tenable
one, repeatedly illustrated by McGinty's rise to the top.
When the Boss offers him the opportunity to be the reform
party's candidate for mayor, McGinty sees the perpetual
corruption of party politics:[15]

> McGinty (Suspicious of a joke): Whata you got to
> do with the reform party?
> The Boss: I _am_ the reform party, who do you
> think?
> McGinty: Since when?
> The Boss: Since a long time. In this town I'm
> _all_ the parties. You think I'm goin' to starve
> every time they change administrations?

Sturges has simplified the situation to a cartoon strip exchange that characterizes the negativism and honesty of his
populism.

Among the screenplays Sturges wrote and directed,
The Great McGinty and The Lady Eve, Sullivan's Travels,
The Palm Beach Story, The Miracle of Morgan's Creek,

and Hail the Conquering Hero most fully illustrate the use
of language to present his feelings and attitudes and to structure his narratives. (My omission of his later films as exemplary of his screenwriting owes to Sturges' own awareness
of the potentials of film as a photographic medium. The
scripts for The Sin of Harold Diddlebock and Unfaithfully
Yours, especially, have a style intrinsic in the slapstick and
lighting [Unfaithfully Yours] which is activated only by the
finished films. The screenplays of The Great Moment and
The Beautiful Blonde from Bashful Bend are either in several
versions, no one truly definitive, or simply poor examples.)
We see, as was noted, Sturges' cynicism throughout McGinty
and his perception of political America as a Tammany Hall
of graft, big bosses, and an essential denial of the fairness
and justice in a democratic system become corrupt. The
comic Sturges, in McGinty and Christmas in July, is an
artist branding his comedy with the scope of his social concerns. In The Lady Eve and The Palm Beach Story, he
deals with comedy as the product of classical drama. The
differences are evident in his characters and their dialogue,
but far more in the structures and traditions of these comedies. The Lady Eve is the masterpiece of the two, forever
spinning complication after complication and leading to a
final reckoning with the admission of love. It is here in The
Lady Eve that Sturges masterminds his most intricate and
original handling of the conventions of dramatic comedy going
back to the Romans.

Sturges' screenplay of a cardsharp in love with a
brewery heir who creates an elaborate set of traps to bring
him into the world he has denied himself--all in the name
of her love--scrambles in wonderful fashion the different
phases of classical comedy. [16] In The Lady Eve, as in The
Palm Beach Story, the episodes of confused identities, principals in romantic pursuit of each other, and an awakening
from the world of pretense or desire to the real world inform the structures of these stories. The Palm Beach Story
resolves all of its complications to the satisfaction of the
comic form; and it is Sturges' conceit, no less, that the
Claudette Colbert twins, the resolution to the plot, are offered to us at the opening of the story. However, The Lady
Eve does much more. Out of his reinforcement of the real
world--the world of Jean and her con artists--Sturges succeeds in proclaiming the romance of illusion as, finally,
just this possible reality.

He starts his screenplay with a fateful apple falling on Charley's head--on Jean's terms--and ends it on her terms, as well, with Jean asking forgiveness and fulfilling her desire for commitment. Here, at the beginning, she sets up her trap with a sarcasm that clearly signals her role as the controlling force in the story, and never in a Sturges film has a role been more disposed toward such control. In a brilliant monologue as she observes Charley, Sturges created a scene totally subjective in point of view, yet fully conscious of using a multiply reflexive camera. Here Charley sits in the ship's dining room absorbed in his book, Are Snakes Necessary?, as Jean observes through her compact mirror the women trying to snare him and his reactions to them. Assessing the moment as she plans her own trap, her thoughts follow:[17]

> Jean: [A woman has just dropped a handkerchief by Charley's table to attract his attention] That's right ... pick it up ... it was worth trying anyway, wasn't it? ... Look at the girl over to his left ... look over to your left, bookworm ... there's a girl pining for you ... a little further ... just a little further. THERE! Now wasn't that worth looking for? See those nice store teeth, all beaming at you. Why, she recognizes you! She's up ... she's down, she can't make up her mind, she's up again! She recognizes you! She's coming over to speak to you. The suspense is killing me. 'Why, for heaven's sake, aren't you Fuzzy Oathammer I went to manual training school with in Louisville? Oh, you're not? Well, you certainly look exactly like him ... it's certainly a remarkable resemblance, but if you're not going to ask me to sit down ... I'm very sorry. I certainly hope I haven't caused you any embarrassment, you so-and-so,' so here goes back to the table. Imagine thinking she could get away with anything like that with me ... I wonder if my tie's on straight ... I certainly upset them, don't I? Now who else is after me? Ah! the lady champion wrestler, wouldn't she make an armful ... Oh, you don't like her either ... Well, what are you going to do about it ... Oh, you just can't stand it any more ... you're leaving ... these women just don't give you a moment's

peace, do they ... Well go ahead! Go sulk in
your cabin! Go soak your head and see if I care.

But Jean, too, is finally exposed and rejected by
Charley. Charley, in fact, runs away from this painful
reality, occasioning the fulfillment of Northrop Frye's identification of the second phase of classical comedy. As Frye
notes: "A more complex irony in this phase is achieved
when a society is constructed by or around a hero, but proves
not sufficiently real or strong to impose itself. In this situation the hero is usually himself at least partly a comic humor or mental runaway, and we have either a hero's illusion
thwarted by a superior reality or a clash of our illusions."18

It is indeed the clash of two illusions that stuns Charley. By leaving, he failed to realize Jean's love for him;
he noticed only her capacity for artfulness. Consequently,
Sturges returns Jean as Eve in a move that is not at all a
comic resurrection, but a further extension of her deceit.
The Jean/Eve duality is characteristic of the classical comedy tradition of doubling, and a feature identified by Frye in
his discussion of the third phase of comedy.19 Here, in the
context of Sturges' romantic comedy, it represents its own
self-fulfilling license, hilariously explained by Eric Blore.
Jean and Eve's relationship, the hidden and apparent sisters
of a ridiculous family scandal, only adds to the intricacy of
the dual relationship. For if Charley cannot have Jean, he
can now have the mysterious embodiment of her called Eve.

The dual identity in The Lady Eve is also a far more
interesting device than the two sets of twins, the Colberts and
McCreas, in The Palm Beach Story. Unlike The Lady Eve,
the identity feature in The Palm Beach Story offers an instant
solution to the complexity it creates. Sturges carries it off
in audacious style, but far less as a measure of compromise
than as the sharp, final, irony, very much like the black cat
and Jimmy MacDonald's contest win at the end of Christmas
in July. In The Lady Eve, however, the incarnation of Eve
seasons Charley for the reappearance of Jean without once
depriving him of his object of romance. Within the limits
of Hollywood morality, Sturges provides his screenplay with
this license as a kind of erotic bigamy for Charley and a
ghoulish infidelity for Jean. Their union in impending marriage suddenly takes on a weird purpose: to teach Charley
a lesson yet to satisfy the desire of both principals to have
each other. From this point in the story, Sturges carries
Jean's "lesson" still further, when, during the train sequence,

Eve disburdens the history of her past affairs to a devastated
Charley. The story has now been brought to another point of
painful reality.

Up to now, Sturges has structured his screenplay as
a metamorphosis of alternating worldly and romantic realities.
From Jean's initial deception and falling in love with Charley
(illusion), Sturges exposed her true identity (reality). From
her reappearance as the mesmerizing Eve (illusion), he had
Charley pay penance in hurt and through Eve's merciless honesty (reality). And now Sturges reunites his principals, Jean
and Charley, on yet a new level of reality, one close to
Frye's description of the fifth phase of comedy as "a world
that is still more romantic, less Utopian and more Arcadian,
less festive and more pensive, where the comic ending is
less a matter of the way the plot turns out than of the perspective of the audience."[20] Charley and Jean have found
each other again and have found from a more mature vantage
point that they need each other. The truth, never fully
known, is now rendered mute and unimportant. For that
which is reaffirmed is what they see of and in each other,
"outraging reality and at the same time introducing us to
a world of childlike innocence which has always made more
sense than reality."[21]

Sullivan's Travels is one of the most unusual and cap-
tivating comedies to come out of Hollywood and has one of
the truly original screenplays concocted out of ego and intro-
spection. Too few screenplays up to that time bear the distinction of originality quite as Sullivan's Travels does, and
the major feature that places it in its own category is its
self-justification as a statement of values within the form of
a sophisticated comedy entertainment. Sullivan's Travels is
a comic odyssey, with its protagonist starting out as little
more than a well-intentioned film director feeling a guilt
about the lack of humane mission in his work. Sturges then
proceeds to bring Sullivan from the world of ignorance to
the realization that he himself is caught in the machinations
of an unfair world. Through this odyssey, he satirizes the
features of the tragic hero while consigning them to his vir-
tuous fool, John L. Sullivan. Sullivan's interest in poverty,
silly and egotistical, will become a serious and irrevocable
involvement in the course that this story will take.

Northrop Frye asks in A Natural Perspective:[22]

The real critical question here is: Does anything
that exhibits the structure of a comedy have to be
taken as a comedy, regardless of its content or
of our attitude to that content? The answer is
clearly yes. A comedy is not a play which ends
happily: it is a play in which a certain structure
is present and works through to its own logical
end, whether we or the cast or the audience feel
happily about it or not.

The opening scene of <u>Sullivan's Travels</u> approaches the brink
of comic acceptance, but retreats when we see that the scene
of the train death is just a movie within a movie. Sturges
establishes different levels of reality beginning with this opening, and the scene will be similarly repeated when Sullivan
embarks on his travels for the second time to learn about
poverty. These scenes are nothing if not multiple illusions
of reality--cinematic comic masks, of a sort--each negating
the one before it with a new perception of what reality must
now be. Hence, Sturges shows us a train-top death to be a
celluloid illusion, a lie, but then also exposes the sham of
Sullivan's world and its pretense to make pictures sympathetic
to human suffering (the scene immediately following in the
screening room). Finally, Sturges places Sullivan himself,
truly helpless, among the have-nots he wishes to understand,
out of his world and without his name.

The seer of this fate is Sullivan's butler played by
Robert Greig, Sturges' comic clown and here one of the
most memorably displayed actors of his stock company. "Occasionally such a character may speak to a focused mood,"
Frye notes, "which gets past the conflict of sympathy and
ridicule, and becomes a direct insight into the comic cathar-
sis itself."[23] The butler's speech is outside the action of
the story, but this perspective suddenly becomes internalized,
"so that we are forced to participate in what we have been
conditioned to think of as removed from us and our sym-
pathies."[24] The butler warns Sullivan:[25]

> Sullivan: I'm going out on the road to find out
> what it's <u>like</u> to be poor and needy ... and
> then I'm going to make a picture about it.
> The Butler: If you'll permit me to say so, sir:
> The subject is not an interesting one. The
> poor know all about poverty and only the mor-
> bid rich would find the topic glamorous.
> Sullivan (Exasperated): But I'm doing it <u>for</u> the
> poor.

The Butler: I doubt that they would appreciate it,
   sir. They rather resent the invasion of their
   privacy ... I believe quite properly, sir. Also,
   such excursions can be quite dangerous, sir. I
   worked for a gentleman once who likewise, with
   two friends, accoutred himself as you have, sir,
   and then went out for a lark.... They have not
   been heard from since.
Sullivan: That was some time ago?
The Butler: 1912, sir. (Then after a pause) You
   see, sir, rich people and theorists, who are
   usually rich people, think of poverty in the negative ... as a lack of riches ... as a disease
   might be called the lack of health ... but it isn't,
   sir. Poverty is not the lack of anything, but a
   positive plague, virulent in itself, contagious as
   cholera, with filth, criminality, vice and despair
   as only a few of its symptoms. It is to be
   stayed away from, even for the purposes of
   study.... It is to be shunned.
Sullivan: Well, you seem to have made quite a
   study of it.
The Butler (Dryly): Quite unwillingly, sir ...

So Sullivan, forewarned, goes to learn about poverty
and Sturges presents two versions of his experience--again,
one layer of reality soon to be supplanted by another more
intense, more accurate and unrelenting version. The first
part of the screenplay contains a series of scenes that find
Sullivan and his female companion (Veronica Lake) trying to
be hoboes, to get a cup of coffee at a roadside diner, and,
later, Sullivan trying to earn money as a handyman. This
is the funny side, the comic illusion, milked for its laughs
and ridiculing a still ignorant Sullivan. Here Sturges includes scenes of slapstick pandemonium and the best moments of his "talk"--wry, sarcastic, and often bullet-
speed--spun on and on at times through the use of his hook
system. One scene of such dialogue exchange, stolen count-
less times by other screenwriters and by television situation
comedy writers, occurs when Sullivan takes some odd jobs
from "Miz Zeffie." She observes the perspiring, bare-
chested Sullivan as she talks to her sister Ursula:[26]

Miz Zeffie (Occupied with her thoughts): You don't
   suppose we're overworking him, do you ... Oh,
   I doubt it ... he seems very strong.

She takes a peek out the window.

> Did you notice his torso?
> Ursula: I noticed that you noticed it.
> Miz Zeffie: Don't be vulgar, dear ... some peo-
> ple are just naturally more sensitive to some
> things in life than some people are.... Some
> are blind to beauty, while others ... are not
> ... even as a little girl you were more of an
> acid type, dear, whereas I, if you remember ...
> Ursula: I remember better than you do.
> Miz Zeffie: Well, forget it ... and furthermore,
> I have never done anything that I was ashamed
> of, Ursula.
> Ursula: Neither have I.
> Miz Zeffie (Charmingly): Yes, but nobody ever
> asked you to, dear.

After Sullivan fails at this orchestrated attempt to be
in the "real" world, Sturges frees him in the world of which
he wishes to learn by a startling twist of the story involving
the theft of his shoes containing his identification. Now Sullivan will enter the reality he has been spared, the reality
of a grim truth. Only after he has been put through the subsequent experiences of this reality, only after being impris-
oned and beaten and put on a chain gang, and only after con-
fessing to a murder he did not commit, will he be redeemed
to a higher awareness that stations him in a final reality.

It is for this reality that Sturges will have exercised
the comedy form in Sullivan's Travels. Here, he states his
affinity for Sullivan's new awareness, a vision so powerfully
felt and represented that it has become indistinguishable from
his own. In this Sullivan, Sturges shows a curious tragicomic
resurrection where Sullivan functions as a kind of Aristophan-
ic protagonist making his second coming, reaffirming his role
as a risen hero by a missionary sobriety to the importance
of making Hollywood comedies.

The stylistic union of dramatic narrative and the film
medium reaches a high point in Sturges' career with The
Lady Eve and Sullivan's Travels and becomes ever more
pronounced in two of his following works: certainly The
Miracle of Morgan's Creek and Hail the Conquering Hero
reflect this and display a remarkable integration of the two.
In Morgan's Creek the script is the framework for the larger

scope of Sturges' satire. And in Hail the Conquering Hero
it delineates the ambivalences represented on a grander scale
in the movie. The screenplays attain prominence here for
the truly transparent quality they achieve as elements of the
film form. It is possible to discuss them apart from the
other elements, but less fruitful; for now the wholly inte-
grated style of Preston Sturges must be reckoned with. These
later screenplays are more complex, mood pieces that sketch
scenes of a disturbing double-edged quality. Even with Sullivan's Travels, there is an unsatisfactory acceptance of Sullivan's awakening when, assembled with his fellow prisoners in
a rural black church, Sturges expiates the cruelties of the
world by projecting Disney cartoons. Pluto, in the face of
reality and in a horribly surreal way, provides the compromise between corruption and innocence, between life and the
cinema.

The comedy deepens in The Miracle of Morgan's
Creek and Hail the Conquering Hero (in Unfaithfully Yours,
it darkens), but so do the consequences. There is a rad-
icalism in Morgan's Creek so seductive that the slapstick
almost appeases it--but not quite. After the local attention
aroused by Trudy's advancing pregnancy, Papa Kockenlocker,
Emmy, and she retreat to the coziness of a quiet Christmas
at home. This is the calm after the storm for them, with
Papa decorating the tree and Trudy, serenely bewildered,
very soon to give birth. A cow swings open the upper part
of the back door in the kitchen, but Emmy thinks nothing of
it. It is the scene where Norval comes to see Trudy to
tell her how sorry he is for everything that has happened
and that he is leaving Morgan's Creek, and it is played to
the soft strains of a Christmas carol. Sturges withheld
nothing from his portrayal of this modern American version
of the Nativity. In a world thriving on the mania of the absurd, he painted a scene so pointedly iconoclastic, so in
deference to its religiosity yet in defiance of the solemnity,
that no Christmas scene has ever matched its power of contemporary appropriateness. Who better than Trudy to mock
the very blessing of virginity? And with a cow at the man-
ger at that.

There is a relentlessness written into a scene like
this: There is no possible way to modify it. It contains
an essential antagonism, a totally unappeased vision.

Sturges considered his screenwriting to be an extension of his playwrighting, the screen being for him the most

vital form for dramatic presentation after the stage. "Your
playwright must have a conflicting opinion for every opinion
he expresses," he said after making Sullivan's Travels, "and
this conflicting opinion must be as good, or nearly as good,
as the opinion which it opposes. It must not be better, however, or matters get out of hand."27 The idea behind this
requisite motivated Sturges' best film work, for it brought
to light his greatest emotional and ideological conflicts. For
every viewpoint, there is its alternative, a contradiction; for
every feeling there is its opposite feeling; for every situation
there is a paradox. Toward the end of Hail the Conquering
Hero, after Woodrow has confessed his hoax, we stand, along
with him, at the crossroads of a precarious narrative development. A crowd carrying signs noisily gathers and the
scene darkens. They approach Woodrow. He faces them,
scared, but suppressing his fear. After a pause, some of
the faces grin with forgiveness: they still want Woodrow.
An angry mob is turned into a group of benevolent supporters.
The density of expression contained in this scene is the para-
digm for the most precious moments of a writer who prodded
the limits of his screenwriting art. There is an elevated
confusion of the mind and of the heart here. Sturges in-
flects his complex response to this moment for the chance
to allow us to feel our humanity a bit more.

WRITTEN AND DIRECTED BY PRESTON STURGES

First Films and Success in America: "The Great McGinty" and "Christmas in July"

The Great McGinty opens with a scene set in a seedy and hostile bar somewhere in a Latin American banana republic. This opening scene sets the tone of Sturges' film in two ways. First, the suggestion of seedy refuge mixed with failure tells us that Sturges is pessimistic about the accredited value of participating in the building of a good, decent brotherhood. And second, this opening scene, with its darker photography creating the visual scape for the entire film, shows us that even in failure, even in exile in a Latin American banana republic, one may not be any worse off than before. Starting over, dismal as the prospect may be and blemished as one has become, begins at the neutral point of great possibilities.

It was exactly at this point that McGinty stepped on the lowest rung of the ladder to political success, and Sturges' film implies that what was possible for McGinty could happen to many of us. But an America envisioned as a nation of great possibilities has never superseded Sturges' understanding of the self-serving inclination of human nature. The Great McGinty, as a political satire, presents a wise, dark, view of humanity, defined visually and verbally in the episodic structure of the story. In McGinty, the visual design is rarely forsaken for the script; indeed, the script to McGinty lacks crispness and breathlessness. Its complexity

On following pages, the two faces of Preston Sturges, the screenwriter and the director, during the filming of Sullivan's Travels, 1941.

is not of the most brilliantly subtle kind found in many of Sturges' other Paramount films.

The episodes structuring The Great McGinty are pointed ironies, lessons in themselves. We see how cleverly McGinty learns to steal votes, we see him discover his own political savvy, we see McGinty choosing to exercise his political upper hand with conscience, and we see the results in his subsequent demise. We see, too, McGinty's succumbing to the kindness and decency of his wife's exhortations. And all these moments, particularly the last one, instruct us in understanding a perspective wary of American ambition.

Sturges used Muriel Angelus, a Scottish actress of the British stage and screen and unknown to American audiences, in the role of McGinty's wife. Catherine presumably inspires the goodness in him, but we have never been convinced that McGinty is truly a bad character. His unkempt manner has suggested instead someone in need of caring and encouragement, of someone to bring out what is essentially there. The idea of the love of a good woman, an otherwise transparent cliché, serves here to prod McGinty into exercising a capacity for good that backfires in the end, and to reveal the alternative side to corrupt politics as that benevolent progressive spirit that is ultimately defeated.

Sturges begins the story of McGinty backward and accomplishes two important feats as a storyteller. First, he removes the suspense required by the climax of mounting plot complications and thus focuses our attention on the matters of attitude and ideological perspective. (Even though McGinty's escape is climactic, it comes after we know he has escaped.) And then, Sturges succeeds in shaping attitude and perspective with a narrative structure. One is a recomposition to the greater service of the other, a more meaningful construction. The point here is to defuse a cold, hard, rather miserable viewpoint in order to turn it into a human parable. Hence, Sturges plays with our standard populist Americanisms about power and politics in his screenplay. When Boss Akim Tamiroff defends his thuggery, he's not so evil, he suggests. After all, he gives protection, he claims, "and good protection, too." "If it wasn't for me," he continues, "everybody'd pick on 'em." And no irony is truer than when William Demarest remarks: "If it wasn't for graft, you'd get a very low type of people in politics-- men without ambition." But Tamiroff captures most pointedly this darker side of the success ethic in American politics

The Boss (Akim Tamiroff) and McGinty (Brian Donlevy) in
The Great McGinty.   "This is a land of great opportunity. "
(The Museum of Modern Art/Film Stills Archive)

when he proclaims to McGinty: "If you keep on like you've
started today there's no telling where you'll be tomorrow.
This is a land of great opportunity. " We understand such
lines and laugh at them with some wisdom.   However, this
forming of attitude that prepares us for the story of McGinty's rise and fall is infected with a more serious proposition:
the display of goodness and decency is the least efficacious
and profitable human measure.   It is often misunderstood and
rarely much appreciated.

     Old-time, big-city-boss politics represents the spirit
of modern America best.   Through Sturges' depiction of the
way such government operates, we understand the historical
implications of a land conceived in the byplay of democracy
and acquisitiveness, of a country existing in a framework of
freedom that, ironically, nurtures oppression.   Sturges' camera observes a gradual acquiescence to such oppression.   His
medium shots observe McGinty's step-by-step climb to the
top, only to expose an irreversible and stupid corruption that
often thwarts its own best purposes.

With this style and largely through this dark mood of detachment, McGinty functions according to the epic standards of Brechtian drama. Our sympathy is constantly met with a disheartenment about the ultimate value of doing good in a preponderantly crooked society. The Great McGinty moves, sequence by sequence, with the blitheness of a lesson being offered--an acrid, comic lesson. For Sturges shows us an indomitable situation, one that cannot be changed (or promise a just change) and must therefore be fled. That one flees to a Latin American banana republic suggests that a greater human reality for Sturges is in one's inclination to look out for one's own skin. In this sense, neutrality, returning to point zero, is the way things are. And, in that, the pessimist would conclude that life should never be expected to be any better than it gets.

The smallness of Christmas in July offers such an unusual concentration of camera, writing, and performing skill that its short running time (sixty-seven minutes) and tiny budget (approximately $353,000) promised a still-untapped inventiveness in Sturges. The camera does more than efficiently photograph its performers; it shows a closeness of people and captures a neighborhood feeling in its affectionate portrait of those who, unlike McGinty, never make it big yet are not failures. Christmas in July never substitutes meagerness for this smallness; and its story of having a chance at personal accomplishment shows that the exercise of individual imagination, as much as profit, motivates such achievement.

Sturges--tinkerer, inventor, businessman, and punster-- has a fondness for Dick Powell's Jimmy MacDonald ("'If you can't sleep at night, it's not the coffee, it's the bunk'--It's a pun! A play on words! Get it?"), and Christmas in July counterbalances the bitterness of The Great McGinty to an extent that the films function as companion works presenting two sides of Preston Sturges. Christmas in July and McGinty reveal conflicting ideas and feelings about an American society structured at the expense and enervation of a success ethic of questionable value. Unlike McGinty, Christmas in July has energy--energy that feeds more energy to show the excitability and mania Sturges captured so brilliantly in Hail the Conquering Hero. The reception for Jimmy as he tells his neighbors, laden with presents for everyone, about winning the Maxford House Coffee Contest anticipates the crowd scenes in Sturges' later Paramount films. And the office sequence early in the story, a statement of impressive

Ellen Drew and Dick Powell (center, in rear) in Christmas
in July. That neighborhood feeling. (The Museum of Modern
Art/Film Stills Archive)

routineness, perfectly displays his talent for congesting and
animating space. The camera pulls back slowly to reveal
a virtual sea of typists working in symmetrical harmony.

   Christmas in July presents an ambivalent view of
America as a place that challenges the ambitious but offers
a dubious reward for such expended energy. Jimmy wants
innocently enough to offer Betty (Ellen Drew) and his mother
(Georgia Caine) the comforts and security they do not have,
but he emerges as a victim of, as much as a testament to,
his society. He wants to prove himself as an advertising
talent, ironically according to those standards fashioned to
appease and vindicate the rich at the expense of the poor.
Here Sturges implies an acceptance of this success ethic,
with some reservation: the ambitious who feed on this energy resent the moneyed class yet are nurtured by its

illusions. When Jimmy and Betty walk across the roof, we hear the strains of "Penthouse Serenade" as they talk of their dreams. This is a sweet and innocent moment of them in leisurely stroll, captured in medium-long tracking shot. And a vulnerable moment, as well, for their hopes and Jimmy's aspirations are precarious at best, and we see at the end of the story that hope prevails only at Betty's imploring. The hoax has been exposed, a dejected Jimmy confesses to Mr. Baxter (Ernest Truex), and she interrupts:

> All he wants ... all any of them want ... is a chance to show ... to find out ... what they've got while they're still young.... Oh, I know they're not going to succeed ... at least most of them aren't ... they'll be like Mr. Waterbury soon enough ... most of them anyway ... but they won't mind it ... they'll find something else, and they'll be happy because they had their chance ... because it's one thing to muff a chance when you get it ... but it's another thing never to have had a chance.

Sturges, who had numerous opportunities to pursue his own varied interests throughout his lifetime, pleads this viewpoint in vilification of the entrapment found in anonymous respectability, in vilification of being a responsible but complacent working stiff. Mr. Waterbury defensively protests earlier in the story that he "is not a failure." "You see," he went on, "ambition is all right, if it works, but no system could be right where only one half of one per cent were successes and all the rest were failures." He is right. However, the point does not dislodge Sturges' perspective. Success in Christmas in July is far more than winning the prize money of a slogan contest; it is the using up of creative ambition, of having the opportunity actively to test one's imagination in a society designed as a competitive marketplace. When Jimmy and Betty are dreaming their dreams together up on the roof, their dialogue is soft and relaxed, the natural banter of two young people in love. The camera follows them as Jimmy talks about accomplishing his goals, and we understand the need to feel the promise of unlimited possibilities. As Sturges himself was to find out, the reality of accepting one's limitations comes soon enough.

With The Great McGinty and Christmas in July, we see Sturges' desire to make a personal imprint in filmmaking through dialogue and camera. The temperament and attitudes

established in these films came to be a part of Sturges' total
vision of a comic-cultural panorama of characters and points
of view.   And although Sturges is a somber comedian here,
he nonetheless functions as a barometer for what makes us
laugh.   This reveals itself more forcefully in his subsequent films.   However, Sturges' directorial career as a whole
was one aggressive movement to touch all the bases of comic
possibilities, and to do so conscious of the heritage of comedy.   Hence, humor erupts from bitterness as well as sentimentality, from sarcasm and gentleness, and from subtle
wryness as much as a pratfall, a joke, a pun, a play on
words.

Christmas in July and The Great McGinty are, in this
sense, a study in light and shadow, an attempt to define this
temperament and its attitudes through a total screen project.
That one film complements the other shows us that Sturges
had yet to integrate ambivalent ideas and feelings into a
complete and sustained work of personal style.   That he attempted it, however, testifies to his commitment to succeed
precisely in that spirit of ambition he examined in these
first works.

"The Lady Eve" and Fabled Lovers

The poetry of the final appeals for forgiveness in
The Lady Eve is accordingly a function of the way
just this man and this woman half walk, half run
down a path of gangways, catching themselves in
an embrace on each landing, and how just this sequence of framings and attractions of the camera
follow these bodies as they inflect themselves to
a halt before a closed door, and just the way these
voices mingle their breaths together.   These moments are no more repeatable than a lifetime is.
The uniqueness of the events of film may be better
thought of in comparison with jazz rather than opera.   Here the point of contact is that the tune is
next to nothing, the performer--with just that temperament, that range, that attack, that line, that
relation to the pulse of the rhythm--is next to
everything.

--Stanley Cavell, "Pursuits of Happiness:
A Reading of The Lady Eve"[1]

Charley Pike knows his snakes, finding their natural habitat a familiar and hospitable home. Eden could not have looked better to him as Sturges' view of man-in-the-wild presents us with a helpless victim of civilization and wealth, spiritually alien to their comforts, pleased with his snakes. For Pike's real devouring jungle is the world of people, and his fall from grace arrives when he reaches their company.

"Snakes are my life," declares a befuddled Henry Fonda as Barbara Stanwyck slithers her fingers through his hair. "What a life!" she gasps, intoxicating him with her effortless seduction. He relents--Stanwyck having edged him off of his seat onto the floor. Our wide-eyed innocent has just experienced his first temptation in Sturges' most classically structured comedy, The Lady Eve. The spirit of his farce originates in subtle irony, sharp wit, and an extraordinary display of verbal brilliance by three actors with a style of casual shrewdness designed to gull the ordinary intelligence: Stanwyck, Charles Coburn, and Eric Blore truly are smart hustlers.

The Lady Eve is a fable on the acquiring of wisdom and the intelligence motivating romantic love. And Sturges, the farceur-director, displays an apparently violent hostility toward innocence (Fonda) that is really more a gesture of desperation, a need to season the object of love because one (Stanwyck) loves him so much. The Lady Eve uses many of the conventions of classical comedy from Plautus to Shakespeare--particularly the convention of identity, which is handled in every way imaginable, from mistaken identity to dual identity to confused identity--and reveals them through a camera style that illustrates how to show such intricately designed dramatic play between characters/actors and the situations in which they are placed. In The Lady Eve, subtleness of gesture--a sharp grin, a crease in Stanwyck's face, or a puzzled glance by Fonda--composed in medium-close two-shot generates the irony intrinsic in Sturges' exquisite dialogue. The camera counterpoints ineptitude (Fonda) with grace (Stanwyck), confusion with order, passivity with aggression, and expresses more clearly than in any of Sturges' work the division between slapstick and buffoonery (Fonda, Eugene Pallette, and William Demarest) and verbal wit and slyness (Stanwyck, Coburn, and Blore). At first glance, the dichotomy appears choppy, each technique isolated; but Sturges attempted and succeeded in doing just the opposite. Complementary comic strategies are necessary in expressing the unlike attitudes and styles of these two personalities who

The Lady Eve. Barbara Stanwyck as Jean protects Henry
Fonda, the object of her attraction, from her father, Charles
Coburn--"as fine a specimen of the sucker sapiens as it has
been my fortune to see." (The Museum of Modern Art/Film
Stills Archive)

are attracted to each other, and this symbiosis appears even
when each responds to the other in reaction shots.

Henry Fonda and Barbara Stanwyck are the sustaining
personalities in this film, and Sturges worked more pro-
ductively with their screen images than those of any other
stars he directed, except possibly Eddie Bracken. The Lady
Eve is reportedly Fonda's and Stanwyck's favorite film, and
one can see why. Fonda's Charley Pike--"Hopsie"--and Stanwyck's Jean/Eve as comic figures also become characters of
human substance and dimension. Pike, laughably charming,
possesses and articulates an acceptance of naiveté that makes
him a reluctant student of the ways of the world. He captivates Jean with genuine affection, however gullible he remains to her cleverness. Indeed, his confession of love on
the deck of the liner provides some of the most helplessly
self-indulgent woo anyone could hope to hear, parodied later

in the movie when he uses it again on Eve. In this later
scene, accompanied by a horse--a crueler symbol of foolish-
ness unimaginable--Charley is indeed in the deeper reaches
of suckerdom, bordering on just this side of credibility.
Perhaps because Sturges brings him to this edge but does
not allow him to fall or look stupid, but merely dumb, can
Charley survive our impending disbelief in his gullibility.
This later confession does not undermine his sincerity, but
reinforces it; for Charley has no bag of tricks. In his case,
it is the repetition of the same emotion felt again and its
point of reference is the original "first time" of that experience. (Fonda specialized in such roles in the late 1930s
and early 1940s. When he played them straight, they were
infused with an extreme sincerity and overriding moral right-
eousness, as in John Ford's Young Mr. Lincoln [1939] and The
Grapes of Wrath [1940]. When they were comic parts, he
became the fabled innocent--not unlike Pike, only less sophisticated. The perfect spoof of Fonda's wholesomeness
and slightly deprecatory style is Walter Lang's 1942 The
Magnificent Dope.)

Stanwyck's Jean /Eve emerges as one of the most
completely constructed women characters in American cinema, her luminousness and self-confidence defining a responsible behavior and permitting the admission of tender feeling
for Charley, for love. Jean's cleverness, her calculating
skill, demand respect, for they are less the product of any
spurious notion of female intractability than an intransigent,
superior, intelligence in action. A moral intelligence as
well, since Jean is willing to unmask herself for love on
the assumption that total honesty is the only respectable behavior toward someone loved. However, Charley finds out
about her past before she confesses her identity and she
encounters the hurt pride of the male ego. "They told me
who you were ... the morning after I met you," he lies.
Jean offered her heart to him and Charley did not realize
the full value of such an offer. Her love is vain and rare,
and he stupidly bypasses it. Consequently, Jean's serpen-
tine transgression upon him as Eve comes from this un-
thinkable refusal to accept her love and the hurt she feels
because of it. And Stanwyck's transformation from Jean to
Eve displays a resolute desire to sensitize this dullard to
the way of love, to make him an object worthy of her love.

It is in this spirit of gamesmanship that The Lady
Eve becomes a chase that makes its principals wise in a
pattern of romantic affirmation. If Charley, hit on the

The Lady Eve. Stanwyck as Eve initiating Charley (Henry Fonda) into the school for hurt lovers.

head by an apple, the "fruit of knowledge," at the beginning of the story, snaps out as from a trance (as Stanley Cavell suggests in his brilliant analysis of the film), it is not to accept Jean on her terms. Hopsie knows of Jean, but cannot know her. For Jean, as the object of his attraction, is precisely to remain the product of his romantic imagination just as Charley must never lose his contrapuntal function in Jean's mind as the possibility for the existence of an essentially unadulterated innocence. That he snaps out of a dream, that both do, comes not as a forsaking of illusion for reality: illusion in The Lady Eve is such reality, located in the romantic mind no less than in its cinematic genesis. At the beginning of the film, Jean observes Charley in captivation through her compact mirror, seeing at once, perhaps, a virgin sucker and the sweetness of lost innocence. We see then that The Lady Eve necessarily exists as part of Sturges' desire to sustain illusion (or reflection, which is its opposite, its result or product), and that such sustenance comes in the acceptance of each other--of each other, in this case, as only one in love can see and accept the other.

A comment on Barbara Stanwyck is in order here, as The Lady Eve--the film, the character, the woman--is also the union of a star and her role in a chamber of constant interaction. Stanwyck has rarely been shown to greater advantage on screen than in The Lady Eve. A star with integrity of character and conveying the spirit of resilience and challenging intelligence, she underscores her independence with erotic implication and modulated vulnerability. Stanwyck's most memorable roles always show these latter virtues in an atmosphere of melodrama and lament, and of foreboding destruction. However, her Phyllis Dietrichson in Billy Wilder's Double Indemnity, Martha Ivers in Lewis Milestone's The Strange Love of Martha Ivers, and Thelma in Robert Siodmak's File on Thelma Jordan never obscured a disturbingly human underside, truthful and not pretty, that always surfaced before the end of the story. And her Mae Doyle in Fritz Lang's Clash by Night suggests a contemporary Nora, less destructive in her selfishness and more anguished and responsible in her behavior. Stanwyck flourishes in The Lady Eve with her full range of powers in motion, releasing a finely honed wit and sense of irony in a performance that helps elevate Sturges' film to the rank of such other great screen farces as Renoir's The Rules of the Game and Bergman's Smiles of a Summer Night.

Sturges assumes the position of a foxy sage in The Lady Eve whose wisdom of people distances him from their foibles, and this is precisely what saves his movie from bitterness. For in The Lady Eve, revenge can indeed be sweet (Jean: "I need him like the ax needs the turkey."), however limited in value the charade ultimately may be. [2] With characteristic libertinism and a stroke of comic perversion, Sturges sacrificed his hero only to return him relatively unsaved. The circle brings Charley back to Jean experienced, more humanized and wiser. But not much wiser. The inevitable beauty in Sturges' fable comes much more in our awareness that this irrationality of the heart manages to find a logical and elegant structure: love, perhaps cruel in our pursuit of it, has form and, finally,

humaneness. When Charley runs into Jean on board the
liner for the second time and admits how much he missed
and loves her and asks her forgiveness, she replies, "The
question is, will you forgive me?"

> Charley: What for?
> Jean: Oh, you still don't understand.
> Charley: I don't want to understand ... I don't
> want to know ... Whatever it is, keep it to
> yourself. All I know is that I adore you, that
> I'll never leave you again ...

Our innocent was put through an obstacle course of love and
came out, still, stubbornly, green.

"Sullivan's Travels"

A film about a Hollywood director trying to make a
picture emerges not only as a personal statement by Sturges,
but, in 1941, as an anomalous film story. Sullivan's Travels
is Sturges' apology; more than that, however, it evolves into
a complex and ambivalent work by an artist whose comic
sensibility is shaped as much by the need for wild comedy as
by the pathos and melodrama it obscures. Sullivan's Travels
remains at once a well-executed commentary on Sturges'
crisis as a comedy director aspiring to make "serious" films
and an unsatisfactory treatise that falls short of its philosophical justification: specifically, that comedy has a therapeutic
value for the desperate have-nots in a socially corrupt world.

Joel McCrea's John L. Sullivan is hardly one of Sturges' alter egoes; Sullivan's travels bring him to an emotional
awareness that Sturges already has. However, the ideological
tension arising during the course of this journey suggests that
Sullivan and Sturges converge intellectually midway in the
story through Sturges' attempt to reconcile his melodramatic
inclinations with his comic aspirations. From the point of
Sullivan's "death" onward, the film gathers its own momentum
for both the character and his author, steered by Sturges
through philosophically precarious waters. The opening sequence of Sullivan's Travels begins with a violent train death
similar to the one later in the film; but in this case it is
only the end of a new socially conscious picture ready for
release. The complexity of this sequence becomes apparent
as we continue to watch Sullivan's Travels. Essentially, we

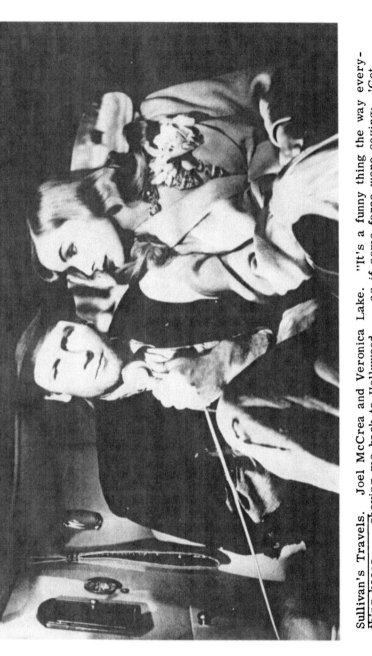

Sullivan's Travels. Joel McCrea and Veronica Lake. "It's a funny thing the way every-thing keeps ... shoving me back to Hollywood ... as if some force were saying: 'Get back where you belong.'"

are only watching a movie and the interpretation rendered in
either sequence arises from our response to the directorial
sensibility at work. When an anonymous anybody is thrown
to his death from the top of a train, we can sigh with surprise, even humor, when we learn that it was only a Hollywood movie shown in a studio projection room. However,
when Sullivan loses his existence, the entire story loses
control, and we respond with apprehension and concern about
his destination--and ours. Where will Sturges lead us?

The first half of Sullivan's Travels could conceivably
be a story in itself: Sully acquires some knowledge about
poverty, and a girl, and will now exercise his righteous intentions by shooting O Brother, Where Art Thou? However,
this part of the film counterpoints the second half in revealing
Sturges' predilection for slapstick, clever dialogue, and carefully written character parts; just as after Sullivan's presumed death, we witness Sturges' sensitivity toward pathos,
sentimentality, injustice, and an acute sense of his own
awareness of being a Hollywood director. But Sullivan's
Travels lacks the gradations between comedy and melodrama;
it switches channels too fast. We feel disconcerted and
sense that the rapid reversal would have been better served
by a transition. The tension operating in Sturges' greatest
comedies, The Miracle of Morgan's Creek and Hail the Conquering Hero, arises from the need to negate the seriousness with laughter, the laughter with seriousness, and, at
moments of brilliance, from how to accept both operating at
once and thus remove, or perhaps heighten, this tension to
a new level. This happens little in Sullivan's Travels. The
only moment when we are thrown off balance occurs when
Robert Greig reprimands Joel McCrea for taking a speculative
interest in the nature of poverty. The camera closes in on
this odd figure of a servant issuing a forbidding warning to
his employer and humor results from the image of a reserved
Victorian butler speaking articulately and authoritatively about
poverty. However, he makes sense, and we are left with a
disquieting feeling which is alleviated only when McCrea tells
Blore, "He gets a little gruesome every once in a while."
To which Blore replies, "... Always reading books, sir."
That last line counterpoints the gravity of the situation and
allays our apprehension of what may be in store for Sullivan.

The uncanny articulateness with which Sturges' stock
company handles itself is a product of incredibly smooth writing that consistently denies pretension. His actors speak
naturally in the best and most controlled fashion, even when

agitated, and what they say surprises us. They comprise a crazy gallery of eccentrics, of people unafraid of letting us know they exist. Porter Hall is the wise-guy promoter impelled to get his words out against Sully's grand aspirations and to express the need to have "a little sex in every picture." William Demarest reappears as Sturges' embodiment of cynical misanthropy. And Esther Howard makes no secret of her lasciviousness. Their lines distinguish them as miniature portraits, allow them to extend or alter the confines of their stereotypes. And this comedy rarely appears cushioned for audience laughter; it originates in the incongruous and sometimes zany situations in which these characters find themselves during the first half of the movie. No one, for example, would expect gruff, burly chauffeur Frank Moran to explain to Sullivan's secretary when a scenarist working on the script of O Brother, Where Art Thou? says:

> Scenarist: 'Thus begins this remarkable expedition into the valley of the shadow of adversity.'
> Secretary: ... 'the shadow of what'?
> Chauffeur: 'The valley of the shadow of adversity' ... It's a paraphrase.

Each one enters the picture briefly, then leaves--but not before making a memorable impression during his time on screen. Consequently, Sturges' repertory attains the brilliance of a cast of minor characters in a Shakespearean comedy: in both cases, the lesser, even bit, roles are delineated with personality and substance.

John L. Sullivan, however, is the most intriguing role in the story, ironically less because he is a carefully wrought character study than as the saturnine device for expressing Sturges' attitudes. He emerges as a testament to Sturges' work not only as a director of comedies, but also as a product of Hollywood, or perhaps a permutation of it. Sullivan is a successful moviemaker--a "boy wonder"--but an unhappy director. In his attempt to be something other than what he is lies a tension with which, in 1941, Sturges may have wrestled. After his second unsuccessful attempt to learn about poverty, a forlorn and exasperated Sullivan remarks, "It's a funny thing the way everything keeps ... shoving me back to Hollywood ... as if some force were saying: 'Get back where you belong.'" The comment implies the paradox of Sturges' own situation as a filmmaker: the constrained energy to create ambitiously outside the Hollywood structure ultimately proved debilitating--nearly destructive--when exercised by a genius that required the studio system to function. The demise became Sturges' own ironic tale, a chapter in his biography operating, in fact, on the intrinsic ironies, one piled upon the other, that kink the course of one's life. Indeed, reading about Sturges' life is much like watching one of his movies: the absurd fatalism, the paradox and irony, become the virtues of a rich and enterprising life.

Sturges' sensitivity toward poverty comes near the end of this first part, in the lyrically orchestrated sequence of McCrea and Lake's adventures in the hobo camps, and illustrates his sense of composition and movement. Sturges understood that projecting realism in the style of King Vidor's social protest works of the 1930s or John Ford's The Grapes of Wrath would have negated any attempt to show sincerely a serious view of life because of the extreme stylistic discordancy it would have created here. Instead, he poeticized the poverty and misery in this sequence, using contrasting lighting and a similarly contrasting soft focus camera to capture faces and silhouetted bodies in motion, and coordinated all of these elements to Sigmund Krumgold's melodramatically stylized orchestration. Sentimentality pervades this sequence as it does the Vidor and Ford films, but here on more acceptable terms. The excesses of it are more authentic, one discovers, than any pretension to document a naturalistic reality about the have-nots in the world would have been. For Sturges' universe defies any notion of such facile reality, if for no other reason than because of the machinations and contrivances of his plots. In Sullivan's Travels, fate, more than realism, allies itself with Sturges' awareness of life. And this attitude is best revealed much later in the film when a bewildered Sullivan, chained to his fellow prisoners, becomes aware of his dead-end predicament and remarks, "If ever a plot needed a twist, this one does"--and then proceeds to give us one by proclaiming himself as the murderer of John L. Sullivan. By some stroke of bad luck, Sullivan landed on a chain gang and, by an added story complication, he is freed. The artist's attitude is clear: fate is the contrivance of life just as Sturges is the manipulator of this picture, never relinquishing his hold on it.

In this light, Sullivan's Travels becomes a blueprint for the concept of cinema storytelling, and Sturges' self-consciousness in plot construction is satirized as much as his story's theme of creative purpose is investigated. Veronica Lake's role is essentially unnecessary to advance the story. She is the implied romantic interest who ultimately justifies her presence by serving as an answer to Sullivan's requisite that "there's a girl in every picture." Cynical and despondent, she serves as devil's advocate to Sullivan's naive desire to make O Brother, Where Art Thou? when she re‑ marks, "There's nothing like a deep-dish movie to drive you out in the open." Under the apparent satire of this comment lie the facts that Sullivan's Travels is not a movie without its deep-dish elements nor one that drove its audiences away.

Sullivan's Travels moves with considerable power on an exclusively visual level as well. For instance, when Sul‑ livan embarks on his initial travels, we see his feet walking first, then the camera pans upward to show us Sullivan in his hobo's costume with the company van following closely behind him. Sullivan's awkwardness, his greenness at pre‑ tending to be poor while being protected by his maternal production crew, comes through without a spoken word. Oth‑ er examples of visual fun appear: the thirteen-year-old jun‑ ior ranger driving his jeep over a hundred miles an hour and the slapstick that results when the trailer tries to follow it; the image of Esther Howard's Miz Zeffie trying to snare Sul‑ livan, and the portrait of her deceased husband frowning sus‑ picion and disapproval upon everyone; the triple bill at the movies (a stab at this silly distribution idea) advertising three melodramas "and SWINGO"--all rely principally on the various visual elements operating in the frame to produce a humorous response. And at the end of the story, when Sullivan con‑ fesses to his own murder, Veronica Lake storms through the studio lot upon seeing his face in the newspaper identified as his own murderer, and the succession of following shots shows the stunned faces of Sullivan's friends and associates. Expe‑ ditiously, Sturges dispenses with verbal exchange in such scenes in favor of a purely visual exposition.

The clever original screenwriting and, more impor‑ tantly, the self-conscious treatment of a story and its pro‑ tagonist make Sullivan's Travels a testament to the extent to which a personal vision could be explored from a Holly‑ wood studio. The grey patina that coats most of Sullivan's Travels becomes a necessary visual correlative to the philo‑ sophical implication of the story: the world cannot be made illusorily pleasant, therefore one must offer human consola‑ tion in whatever form one can. This makes life bearable: it finally answers Sullivan's question, "How can you talk about musical comedies when the world is committing suicide?" Sturges' most personal works, The Miracle of Morgan's

Sullivan's Travels. Joel McCrea and Veronica Lake: the comedy of poverty.

Creek and Hail the Conquering Hero, were lighted by John Seitz; and like the endings in them, the one in Sullivan's Travels does not resolve any of the questions it raises. The dullness in tonal variations, from a washed-out white to a deep grey, and a general lack of soft focus belie any completely happy endings in these works. Their stories are told, but, as in Sullivan's Travels, too much occurs before the end to convince us that every complexity Sturges raises in his

films was penetratingly thought through. <u>Sullivan's Travels</u>
posits no solutions to the socioeconomic inequities it exposes;
it simply tries to vindicate Sturges' desire to make us laugh
in their midst.

"The Palm Beach Story"

Sex has rarely been more sophisticated or more
adroitly presented as a topic of comedy than in <u>The Palm
Beach Story</u>, one of Sturges' most deftly written comedies.
Unlike Ernst Lubitsch's subtle sexiness that often arises
from the allusions to events occurring behind closed doors,
Sturges' treatment of "Topic A" is unabashedly straightfor-
ward, honest, and, in the case of Claudette Colbert's Geraldine Jeffers, extremely practical. In <u>The Palm Beach
Story</u>, sex takes its place alongside greed, ambition, and
leisure-class pleasures, and with no negative connotation
implied. On the contrary, Sturges exposes the fraud of
confusing love with sex and sex with love, and, in doing
so, suggests what in Hollywood at the time was a radical
premise: that one can love another yet sleep with still
another.

Geraldine has an intelligent, reasonable, attitude toward her situation as a married woman who quite frankly
admits that she wants security and comfort, and that love
alone cannot furnish them. Hardly a startling attitude, it
nonetheless becomes refreshingly cogent in Sturges' film,
a product of 1942 Hollywood. The attitude is reinvented in
the context of modern American society and, ironically,
promulgated through a studio system that frowned upon it.
Topic A, as Sturges presents it, casually departs from the
idea that sex acquires respectability in marriage. <u>The Palm
Beach Story</u> proffers the benefit of marriage as a form of
license, not unlike a protective passport or visa, that allows
Gerry to acquire wealth and is easily manipulated by the Princess Centimillia to accommodate her lechery.

Geraldine is hardly reprehensible in her desire to marry for money; she is simply aware of herself as a woman
existing in a particular society. And since she is a poor
homemaker, has no marketable skills, and admittedly is not
much good at anything, her power lies in her attractiveness.
So when Tom fears that sex might have entered into the
wienie king's generosity toward her, she wisely acknowledges,

"Sex always has something to do with it...." But Tom's
ignorance about Gerry's awareness of being a sex object and
his insensitivity toward her dilemma as a woman who understands that if she doesn't look out for herself no one else
will, becomes the inevitable, unappeasable difference that
leads to their temporary separation. Sex has everything yet
nothing to do with it. When Gerry proposes to remain faith-
ful to him, Tom simply cannot understand "what a long-legged
girl can do without doing anything." Yet Sturges plays both
sides of the fence in exposing marital foibles in The Palm
Beach Story, so that when Gerry unconvincingly tells Tom
that he should think of her as a sister, it is clear that Tom
has other ideas about how to treat his wife. Hence, Geraldine's self-awareness, intelligent as it is, requires her to
ignore Tom's love for her and, more importantly, hers for
him.

That sex has such a commodity value in The Palm
Beach Story is not degrading, nor does Gerry humiliate herself in accepting it that way. Sturges offers sex as a mor-
ally detached function of pleasure as well as a function of
love and shows the complications that develop in attempting
to separate the two. The crucial feature of the latter function lies, of course, in the envelopment of sex by personality, and the romantic expression of sex in The Palm Beach
Story is projected only through the personalities of Tom and
Geraldine, but not through those of Hackensacker and the
Princess. Indeed, Mary Astor's Princess Centimillia maintains the most unsentimental attitude toward marriage. For
her, there is nothing else but Topic A and marriage is simply a convenient setup in which to enjoy it. After being "married three times and annulled twice," she realizes that "nothing is permanent in this world ... except Roosevelt."

Sturges was able to manipulate the personalities of
his most important actors with the kind of artistic control
few other directors were able to exercise. He rarely used
big name stars, but that hardly diminished his ability to develop and/or spoof the screen personalities of Barbara Stanwyck and Henry Fonda in The Lady Eve, Joel McCrea and
Veronica Lake in Sullivan's Travels, and particularly a lesser-
known actor like Eddie Bracken in The Miracle of Morgan's
Creek and Hail the Conquering Hero. In The Palm Beach
Story, McCrea displays some of the same innocence and
muscular vulnerability he did in Sullivan's Travels. Whereas
Eddie Bracken registers as a writhing, neurotic bundle of
nerves in Morgan's Creek and Conquering Hero, McCrea's

pratfalls, much like Fonda's in The Lady Eve, arise from
Sturges' cruel need to hurt him--to goad him into wising up
about the apparently limited financial rewards of his inventions and to awaken him to the intelligence of Gerry's argument, not so much because it is a solution to their marital
problem, but because she makes a sensible point. It serves
him right to fall down a flight of stairs and trip along the
way as he tries to retrieve her at Penn Station.

Claudette Colbert's appeal comes from the extraordinarily humane manner in which she interprets the part of
Geraldine. Not potentially hard or manipulative like Stanwyck's Jean, she also projects the opposite image of fraz-
zled, scatterbrained Trudy Kockenlocker. Nor is she bitter
and despondent like Veronica Lake's "girl" in Sullivan's
Travels. Colbert's Gerry strikes a perfect balance between
emotion and logic, and without losing her sense of humor.
She truly knows of her love for Tom, but also understands
what she must do for their welfare. Any vague promises
he offers about future success simply will not suffice, since,
as Gerry realizes, "men don't get smart as they get older,
they just lose their hair."

If Sturges' films reveal a perverse delight for anything, it is a Shavian predilection for names--names like
Kockenlocker, Swandumper, Mayor Noble, Reverend Upperman, "Ratziwatzki," Truesmith, Hickenlooper, Ginglehooper,
and Hackensacker. They, of course, spoof the idea of odd
names as well as the people they identify. Hence, not only
is J.D. Hackensacker III a thinly gauzed parody of Rockefeller, but the actor who plays him, Rudy Vallee, emerges
in his own right as a victim of some of the nastiest lam-
pooning in any Sturges film. Hackensacker--"Snoodles" to
his sister, the Princess Centimillia--becomes at once a
parody of eccentric wealth and of Vallee's own constipated
stolidity. Sturges attacks him from the start, physically
and verbally, as Colbert steps on his face as she attempts
to make her way up to her upper berth, shattering the trademark of his public image, his pince-nez, not once but twice.
However, Vallee, the picture of orderly conservatism, always carries a spare pair. Poor Hackensacker's dilemma
remains unresolved throughout the story: he is so helplessly
trapped by his silly proprieties that he cannot express his
emotions to Gerry. He habitually records figures but never
adds them up. He inherited a yacht that wouldn't be worth
a nickel to him if he had to buy it. He never tips more
than a dime and maintains that tipping, like staterooms, "is

un-American. " Hackensacker is a ridiculous perversion of the very rich; having been born into big money, his sensitivity to other people's need for it has petrified. He has so much money that if poor Gerry could just have $99,000 of it, Tom could realize the start of his architectural dream, an absurd idea to net a part of the city with an overhead airstrip.

Vallee's Hackensacker is a kind, harmless eccentric in Geraldine's eyes, yet Sturges mercilessly persists in ridiculing his image. At one point, when Hackensacker attempts to woo Gerry by singing "Isn't It Romantic?," she responds, "My you have a nice little voice. "--the ultimate insult to Vallee the crooner; the insult is exacerbated when he serenades her later that night, singing "Good Night Sweetheart" below her window while Tom seduces her inside. This sequence illustrates the witty comic strategy worked into the narrative structure of The Palm Beach Story. From the beginning, the film inverts the typical storytelling order by showing a lot of confusing business involving two Claudette Colberts, the inevitable comic resolution and the answer to everyone's problems, and telling us that "they lived happily ever after. " Then Sturges proceeds to start the story by questioning our easy acceptance of this premise with: "... or did they?"

Mistaken identities, misunderstood motives, ironic episodes, and ignorance that leads to further complications are the structural elements of dramatic comedy going back to Shakespeare and deriving from the New Comedy of Menander. Sturges uses them in The Palm Beach Story, and although the structural complexities have this dramatic heritage, they also have a cinematic one reflected in the profuse physical comedy reminiscent of the Keystone Cops. The incredible wienie king, conveniently deaf at the right moments, may be seen as the zany, just as William Demarest and his fellow Ale and Quail Club members are recognizable buffoons. Although he does not mimic any of the leading characters, the wienie king certainly mocks anything they have to say--indeed, the idea of any coherent conversation--by simply not hearing them. In many of Sturges' other films, people refuse to listen to one another. The ultimate absurdity in The Palm Beach Story is this character who cannot hear and consequently distorts what they say, but to no greater confusion than the Ale and Quail Club babblers who wreak havoc with every misunderstood challenge to violence they make to one another. Here, however, the precise comic timing of the wienie king's delivery and the violent slapstick of the Ale

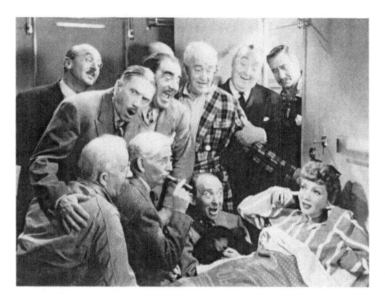

The Palm Beach Story.   The Ale and Quail Club--Sturges'
stock company--sings Claudette Colbert to sleep.

and Quail Club's railroad car "hunt" are the stuff of movies.
The dialogue is too fast and the action too chaotic, too defiant of proscenium confinement.

      Sturges' dialogue style sounds particulary theatrical in
its literateness and in the articulation it demands.   Not only
do Tom and Geraldine carry on wittily, but Hackensacker's
conversations with her are brilliantly intricate speeches, comedy pieces in themselves, smoothly delivered.   At one junc-
ture, he concludes a nimble but long-winded dialectic on dishonorable behavior by observing: "That's one of the tragedies
in this life ... that the men who are most in need of a beat-
ing up ... are always enormous."   The fully potent funniness
of such lines defies explication out of the context of the mood
and moment in the picture; but delivered nonstop by Sturges'
actors/characters, this dialogue, this "talk," becomes the
distinctive imprint of his dense verbal comedy style.   The
personalities fixed on screen and the words they say reveal
the necessary complement of the visual and verbal, a harmony in which Sturges' actors invade the dialogue and give
it the uniquely peculiar expression it deserves.

The Palm Beach Story offers us all the elements of Sturges' style, many of which are most completely synthesized in The Miracle of Morgan's Creek and Hail the Conquering Hero. The story here approaches them in its frenzied pace and plot dynamic but appears deliberate in its execution. Sturges' schematic use of the elements of dramatic structure has him, one senses, happily absorbed in contriving his story. Yet the transcription of story into screen action reveals much more than rigor. Sturges' characters continue to fill the frame, moving excitedly from one train car to another in a constantly murky world. Victor Milner, Lubitsch's cameraman, lighted his films much more brightly than The Palm Beach Story. The difference distinguishes a continental wink (Lubitsch) from a sarcastic grin (Sturges), since Milner's photography is not much brighter in this film than John Seitz's is for Morgan's Creek or Conquering Hero. (Indeed, even Christmas in July and The Lady Eve, both lighted by Milner, maintain that grey haze that permeates Sturges' entire oeuvre except The Beautiful Blonde from Bashful Bend, his only color film, and, arguably, his last film, The Notebooks of Major Thompson.) Perhaps the ending of The Palm Beach Story interprets it best: the optimism implied by a traditional happy ending concluding with marital bliss is a fabulous fabrication for Sturges. He brought his story full circle, exposed the twins, and unraveled the complications, but left us right back where we started: "Everyone lives happily ever after ... or do they?"

"The Miracle of Morgan's Creek"

Poor Norval emerges as a writhing, vulnerable, and gullible mass of right-minded angst manipulated by Sturges in this, his densest and most brilliant film, to reveal the unrelenting misery that befalls someone acting as a caring and loving human being. Norval's innocence and unequivocal sincerity are his "tragic" flaw in a universe operating on an inversion principle that defies our preconceptions about individuals and society. If the world of Morgan's Creek is a topsy-turvy one, it is only because Sturges' ostensibly inhumane attitude toward his characters is really nothing but an almost absurd, lop-sided form of humanity that we display toward each other. Norval emerges as a kind of hero at the end of the story; although he is responsible for nothing (i.e., Trudy's pregnancy), he becomes responsible for everything. A highly respected cultural, much more than biologi-

cal, phenomenon has reaped its harvest six-fold and Norval
is brought back to smoke the cigar for it.

In The Miracle of Morgan's Creek , Sturges' vision of
small-town life in 1940s America affirms certain cultural
myths and values as much as it debunks others. The idyllic
harmony one envisions about provincial America becomes
little more than a delusion in the chaotic world of Morgan's
Creek. All of the same elements are there--the setting,
people, and activities; however, they are constituted differ-
ently, invested with the qualities of frenzied anxiety, contradiction, and paradox.

Trudy Kockenlocker and Norval Jones become the absurd representations of the American home-town boy and his
girl-next-door. Betty Hutton's Trudy, an exuberant blonde
who quite unabashedly loves the company of men, perverts
our stereotyped notion of the demure virgin who waits for
romance and marriage. She is too busy making things happen for herself, having fun with "men in uniform," to care
about marriage. She is fickle, shortsighted, and rather
dumb, and Trudy's selfishness and initial insensitivity to
Norval's affection for her arise less from any despicable
cruelty than from a total disregard for proper, conventional
behavior. Norval's desire to domesticate her simply will
not work; Trudy is too irrepressibly, irresponsibly friendly
with other men to want to take him seriously. And bleary-
eyed, devoted, Norval suffers because of her behavior.

Eddie Bracken's Norval Jones is Sturges' tensest and
most ambivalent protagonist. Norval craves order in his
life--ideally, sharing it with Trudy--but his hyper-dysfunc-
tional behavior belies any possibility for physical, let alone
mental order. His implicitly sexual physical crisis establishes him as one of the most dementedly beautiful examples
of manhood ever to appear in American movies; for it is
with Norval's character that Sturges most effectively deflates,
or inverts, our notions about masculinity. Norval is the
town's 4-F exemption--almost a mascot, of sorts--and the
nervous condition that kept him out against his wish implies
a questionable virility. ("Every time they start to examine
me ... the spots!") Yet, ultimately, ironically, he is the
one who must face the dubious joy and most assured horror
of fatherhood. His dilemma comes as Sturges' critical response to the celebration of such masculine achievement, and
it strangely suits Norval to illustrate it. The schnook who
couldn't cut it with the loose girl-next-door, who couldn't
get into the service, suddenly becomes a symbol of power-

The Miracle of Morgan's Creek.   Betty Hutton and Eddie
Bracken--Trudy and Norval, the transpositions created in
a world where the functions of its basic institutions have
gone awry.

house manliness--and, of course, for the wrong reasons.
Norval's image arises from circumstances for which others
make him responsible: i.e., Trudy's pregnancy. His real
virtues of courage, sincerity, and veracity fight against this
tide of deception and are quite beside the point in assessing
his public image.

Hence, the paradox between intention and appearance
becomes a crucial issue in Morgan's Creek as it does later
in Hail the Conquering Hero. In Conquering Hero, the hero
confesses his charade and Woodrow's honesty and sincerity
become attributes. In Morgan's Creek, however, the deception persists, and wins, over Norval's attempts to expose it,
and does so to the extent of completely guffawing at our honoring of male potency. Indeed, it incongruously befits jittery
Norval to be taken as the sire of, not one, but six babies.

Norval and Trudy are the transpositions created in a world where the functions of its basic institutions have gone awry. Trudy and Emmy, hardly the products of a harmonious household, defy the image of a traditionally unified family. Not only is Papa Kockenlocker brusque with his daughters, but he has no qualms about motioning to strike them in a fit of rage, nor they him. And at one point when he attempts to shoot Norval, they pounce on him, knock him down and pin him to the porch floor with a wrestling hold. Trudy and her sister, too aware of their father's temperamental nature, find it easier to conspire against him, to keep things from him, and, in general, to maintain a lack of communication with Papa than to face him at the risk of possible violence. We see here a sort of family unity based on surliness, concealment, and as much physical as emotional contact--a unity completely antithetical to that of the idealized American family.

The whole setup allows Sturges to execute his predilection for pratfalls, slapstick comedy arising more from a physical attitude of manic discordancy than from carefully crafted sight gags. For Sturges, the art of slapstick is less a matter of the mind exercising control over the body than a case of making one's convulsiveness conform to the desires and intentions one would like to express. Physical movement, in this sense, necessarily plays against linear, logical thinking and undermines such thinking to make us see that the comedy of an orderly existence lies precisely in our dogged attempts to make such an existence possible. Eddie Bracken, the greatest expositor of Sturges' physical comedy, convulses throughout Morgan's Creek and does so best during those critical moments when the greatest deceit is expected of him. Norval's decision to pose as "Ignatz Ratziwatzki" helps Trudy out of her jam, but creates his totally flappable posture that, coupled with his stuttering, practically qualifies him for straitjacketing. Even in quieter moments, his physical disarray forebodes the complications that follow, and Norval simply cannot maintain a slick composure in the face of such adversity; it goes against his grain and would operate against Sturges' anarchic spirit.

This attitude allows Sturges to assault our hallowed institutions, but without proposing their dissolution. The chaos is rooted less in the annihilation of social values than in the belief that they should be shaken up, exposed for their inadequacies as much as for the reasons why we want them. Norval has always wanted to be married to Trudy because

The Miracle of Morgan's Creek.   At left, William Demarest,
Eddie Bracken, and Georgia Caine.

he has always loved her.   Marriage for him was originally
envisioned as a perfect situation, the unattainable dream of
a lifetime.   Trudy kills such an illusion, however, turning
it into a totally unsacred and fickle act.   Marriage is that
incidental detail that becomes the burdensome crux of her
problem, and when Trudy remarks to Norval that she "can't
keep on marrying people, no matter how sweet they are,"
it finally, however shallowly, strikes her that her dilemma
is very much of her own making.   As Emmy points out to
her, "It only costs two dollars to do it."   And Trudy paid
the price to enjoy the pleasure of marriage only to discover
that "some kinds of fun last longer than others."

All these events take place in Morgan's Creek in the
state of McGinty, and Sturges' comments on small-town life
sound bitter, expressing perhaps the perplexing attitude of
an artist who opted for a picture of the zanier side of American life.   Sturges presents us here with a dual viewpoint of

small-town residents as easily excitable people hungry for
notoriety as well as gentle and concerned friends sympathetically offering their support.   So when Emmy consoles Trudy
and advises her not to tell Papa about her pregnancy, she
expresses Sturges' problematical position about such small-
town life.   She comments:

> No one's going to believe something good if they
> can believe something bad. ...   You don't know
> what to expect in a town like this, a town that
> can produce schnooks like Papa ... always sus-
> picious and suspecting the worst in everything.

The tension arises from what Emmy says, as opposed to
what we see.   Sturges' long tracking shots of Morgan's Creek
do not satirize but impassively take note of the various images of small-town life.   And since the characters are a
representative admixture of people found most everywhere,
this biting cynicism stems equally from Emmy's contrapuntal
function in the story.   If she is an overly-wise and sardonic
fourteen-year-old, it contrasts Trudy's naiveté as a twenty-
year-old.   Emmy remains unfettered and sufficiently alert to
help Trudy, while Trudy cannot think and act to help herself.
She becomes, in short, the logical contradiction of her sister
Trudy, and deriding small-town life is less a perception of
its character than a function of hers.

Diana Lynn's role is, in fact, an exemplary voice for
Preston Sturges, the wisecracker.   Subtlety is hardly an effective quality in a world where people come into the picture
then leave it at such a fast pace that each must fight the
others in order to speak his mind.   Speech at this density
becomes a challenge to brisk, wry frankness and articulate
argument.   Here, we have Al Bridge, as the lawyer Mr.
Johnson, expounding his attitude toward marriage (an interesting comparison to what we see in The Palm Beach Story):

> The responsibility for recording a marriage has al-
> ways been up to the woman; if it weren't for them
> marriage would have disappeared long since.   No
> man is going to jeopardize his present or poison
> his future with a lot of little brats hollering around
> the house unless he's forced to.   It's up to the wom-
> an to knock him down and hog-tie him and drag him
> in front of two witnesses immediately, if not sooner.
> Any time after that is too late.

An ironic assertion, since it has been Norval who has always wanted to marry a resisting Trudy, it also reveals the inherent paradox in the narrative preoccupation of Sturges' film. It matters less in Morgan's Creek that marriage may not be a viable institution than that people pursue it. The questionable happiness resulting from it evades Trudy and Norval, for the idea of marrying in Morgan's Creek arises as an immediate solution to the problem of marriage. The only way to legitimize Trudy's marriage to "Ratziwatzki" is for her to marry Norval; it becomes her attempt to conform socially, to absolve her disgrace.

Other moments of character roles in the foreground include:

Georgia Caine, as Mrs. Johnson, expressing her particular maternal instinct: It is Christmas Eve, and confused, desperate, Norval has just escaped from jail and gone to Mr. Johnson's house to inform him with great self-pity that he plans to leave town and never return. As he departs, slowly, sorrowfully, Mrs. Johnson sympathetically asks: "Oh Norval, wouldn't you like to take some fruit cake with you?"

Growling Frank Moran, the M.P., sandwiches in his understanding of how short-tempered Constable Kockenlocker should treat rowdy servicemen in 1942, when he notes: "We do it different now, Ed. It's all done with kindness ... Get the idea? It's more psychological."

While the congestion of crisp dialogue is the single most effective element in Morgan's Creek, much of this verbal barrage occurs during hectic, even violent, sequences and is best seen as a part of the synthesis of the two. In Morgan's Creek, verbal wit never recedes, but neither does the action in a world perpetually in motion. And even when Norval is not stumbling, or Papa taking spills, or Trudy dancing with every G.I. in sight, the quieter moments are covered with that patina of Paramount grey that has become part of Sturges' visual style, that haze through which all his characters move. The studio look notwithstanding, John Seitz's photography in Morgan's Creek becomes a necessary device in our understanding of how to apprehend Sturges' subject. It is less a matter of accentuating or coloring the story through a particular visual emphasis than of maintaining a neutral (not too blanc, not too noir) background which tones the literateness and does not adumbrate the action.

This hardly diminishes the value of his camera since, even without dialogue, Sturges displays wit in visual style that sustains and even advances the narrative without any loss of sensibility. When Trudy is in labor, we see the nurse running with increasing frenzy for blankets after each delivery. We know about her sextuplets before anybody speaks of them, just as we see the overwhelming impact of Trudy's "miracle" when Sturges cuts to shots of international headlines of the event and images of Hitler and Mussolini silently screaming in rage. Without a word, he has illustrated the sensational attention we give to extraordinary events--an attention nothing short of a maniacal response that propels the lunacy in Sturges' world.

Sturges' lop-sided perspective on masculinity, womanhood, birth, marriage, home and small-town life, and other concepts of human behavior and social institutions resonates with clear truth. If we choose to accept certain ideas of their stability, why should Sturges not present us with alternative images? This is not so much an iconoclasm on his part as an examination of the other side of the coin. The extent to which Norval is a spoof of macho or Trudy disregards domesticity is as palpably real in Sturges' world as the matronly, fur-trimmed fat lady who plays a trombone at the servicemen's dance in the church basement, or a banker named Tuerck, or the image of two daughters wrestling with their father. All of this becomes acceptable in Morgan's Creek. And if we understand the contradictions inherent in American life, such a depiction makes peculiar sense. It implies, in the broadest sense, that Sturges utilized Hollywood as a tool to complicate, cynicize, as well as contradict, the myths and vision of America that directors such as Capra, Ford, and Griffith propagated, and to do so in a vital manner that was an alternative style to the concentrated metaphors of Ford's static camera or the rustic peacefulness of much of Griffith's Americana. The kinetic impact of Sturges' compositions--confused crowds pushing their way across the screen and the pratfalls of his convulsing protagonists resolutely driven toward some destination or destiny--belie the delusion that there is much harmony in the world. The frenetic determination of Norval Jones heralds an oddly tolerable, even likable, kind of American angst. It may well be a hyperbolic reflection of our national temperament.

Complexity in Storytelling: Notes on
"Hail the Conquering Hero"

Complexity in narrative cinema becomes a reflexive
issue; for in describing a film as complex, one must illustrate a definition for complexity.   How does a film achieve
or contain it?   And more important: What is the nature of
complexity in a work of narrative cinema?   Much theoretical
discussion has focused on these issues, but certain percep-
tions by V. F. Perkins in his book, Film as Film, become
especially cogent.   As Perkins suggests, complexity in narrative film arises from the subtlety and through the pattern
of detail built over and around the (cruder and often blatant)
asserted meaning(s) of the story, "in an organization of details whose relationships simultaneously complicate and clar-
ify the movie's viewpoint. "3   For a director such as Renoir,
the inexorably long tracking and panning shots that express a
basic reverence for the awareness and flow of life are the
major stylistic dialectic that reveals a complexity of narrative structure through character relationships, ambiguous attitudes, and philosophical perspective.   The extended shots
of Boudu Saved from Drowning and The Crime of Monsieur
Lange, for instance, reflect a narrative, political, and,
above all, humanistic point of view lending itself to a de-
tailed analysis that can mine the richness of these works.
It is a task of unraveling to discuss Renoir's personality
in, say, The Rules of the Game.   The artist synthesized
cinematic technique, dramatic structure, and a personal
vision into a manifold work of art.   It becomes possible to
discuss separately and completely the functions of Renoir's
camera movement, the influence of Beaumarchais and French
farce, and the pessimistic, and sad, commentary on the social malaise in the story as they appear in The Rules of the
Game.   Each function is analyzable apart from the others,
yet operates to complicate the others.   It is the kind of
complexity that creates the tone and what we recognize as
the style of Renoir's work.

Sturges sustains a comparable complexity in a film
that never settles down, one that is in constant flux, attempting to baffle us at every turn of the story with a new
meaning that negates or complicates the one we accepted
just a moment before.   Hail the Conquering Hero is a
smoothly, almost unconsciously, rigorous exercise in narrative cinema.   The acute awareness of narrative structure
revealed in Sullivan's Travels arises as the artist's intuitive

understanding of the screen's particular affinity for storytelling in Conquering Hero. Sturges reveals an extraordinary
ambiguity of purpose and mood in Hail the Conquering Hero,
and complexity arises from his ambivalent feelings and ideas
on an array of topics, and the way storytelling for him
emerges as a reflection of personal conscience as much as
it does as a comedy entertainment.

"Home to the Arms of Mother," the innocent sentiment expressed in the song and in the movie, becomes the
running theme throughout Conquering Hero. Woodrow's
pathos stems precisely from this dilemma: he cannot go
home to the arms of his mother, or his former sweetheart,
or to the outstretched arms of his home-town folk. The
respiratory "excitement" induced by his hay fever kept him
out of the service and he had been living a lie for everyone
back home, particularly for his mother, the widow of war
hero "Hinky Dinky" Truesmith. Losing her respect and pride
is one of the several major concerns Woodrow faces. What
we see as a guilt-ridden depression in Woodrow, however,
manifests itself in one of the most pronounced mother com-
plexes in American film history, in ex-middleweight boxing
champion Freddie Steele's performance as Bugsy, one of
Woodrow's marine pals. (James Cagney's Cody Jarrett in
Raoul Walsh's White Heat offers the classic example.) Bugsy's obsession illustrates most clearly the tension between Sturges' sympathetic acceptance on the one hand, and maniacal
depiction on the other, of a cultural value. Woodrow's af-
fectionate concern for his mother is as touching as Bugsy's
is crazy, and we are left questioning the merits of "mom-
ism." Indeed, it is Bugsy's crackbrained phone call to Mrs.
Truesmith that perpetuates the fraud and puts Woodrow at the
mercy of an ever-increasing deceit.

Woodrow only wants to wallow in his guilt, to deceive
no one any further than he already has. But Sergeant William Demarest simply will not permit it, and Woodrow is
swept up in the madness of townspeople who, delirious in
their excitement, await his arrival. Woodrow, like Norval
Jones in Morgan's Creek, has "greatness thrust upon him"
and no one, his marine buddies or home-town friends, will
allow him to forget his courage. He inverts our notion of
the classic hero who lives to the point of tragic self-
awareness by so clearly knowing his dilemma and fearing its
only solution. Woodrow's weakness--his hay fever--unknown
to the folks back home, becomes the knowledge they must
acquire; it is the operable device that can unravel the "trag-
edy."

Hail the Conquering Hero: Woodrow caught between the
deceived and the deceivers. Harry Hayden, Jimmy Conlin,
Franklin Pangborn, Ella Raines, Freddie Steele (background),
Eddie Bracken, William Demarest (background), Georgia
Caine, Jimmie Dundee and Elizabeth Patterson. (The Muse-
um of Modern Art/Film Stills Archive)

Ignorance alone, however, hardly characterizes Sturges' citizenry. Jumping the gun, a specialty of his characters, becomes the self-imposed myopia of this crowd of
people who simply refuse to listen to one another, and the
result becomes increasingly mired and chaotic as Woodrow
tries to save face and retain his sanity at the same time.
Consequently, he becomes a "hero" in the craziest of fashions, and the more he resists his "heroism," the more it
increases.

Sturges presents us here with a world--his very personal society--of familiar faces and characters that appear
and reappear in every film he made during most all of his
directorial career. His stock company is a gallery of cinematic personalities, and, unlike a theatrical company, Sturges' actors rarely play roles unsympathetic to their natural
inclination to come across as themselves.[4] The crucial

value of the players in Conquering Hero to the organic whole
of this world is best understood in terms of the narrative he
tells. It seems an obvious point to note, but Sturges peoples
his films instead of casting them, and the distinction lies in
the ways he uses actors. Memorable character actors like
William Demarest, Esther Howard, Al Bridge, Elizabeth Patterson, Torben Meyer, Jimmy Conlin, Georgia Caine, Raymond Walburn, and others become etched in Sturges' vision
of America in much the same way that Ward Bond, Dorothy
Jordan, Ben Johnson, and Victor McLaglen reside in John
Ford's western frontier. They grow with each successive
movie and breathe the life of the artist in each work. Other
directors, like Howard Hawks and Alfred Hitchcock, rarely
used their supporting actors to much greater end than to
punctuate the main narrative line with brief interludes, rele-
vant but outside the main flow of the story. Sturges, on the
other hand, allows his players to define themselves, to per-
form for us, and the difference lies between limiting and
liberating minor screen characters. For Hawks and Hitchcock, two great storytellers, the plots grow and move with
comparatively few characters. (Hawks's rarely number more
than six.) For Sturges, the plots are propelled by and, in
this sense, exist for, all his characters: these people constitute the fabric of his narratives.

The absurdity of heroism in Hail the Conquering Hero
is rooted less in satire than in Sturges' understanding that
we invest heroic attributes upon our sacred cows for the
ecstatic pleasure it gives us to believe in the idea of heroism. He hardly derides the possibility for true heroism; he
only laughs at our creation of golden lambs which we delude
ourselves into accepting as heroic gods. After all, the one
fact Woodrow Lafayette Pershing Truesmith has accepted is
that for him heroism must be a way of life, like the son
who inherits the family business, long the feature of genera-
tional pride.

Woodrow Truesmith is the "hero" of the story, but
his heroism and compassion are quite tame, quite vulnerably
human, in view of the grotesque reflections we see of his
virtues in the behavior of those around him--his mother, the
town's hyped-up residents, Evvy Noble, and even Libby.
Mother love, war heroism, political integrity (or any kind,
for that matter), and romantic love are simultaneously ad-
mirable yet torturously inhuman burdens to bear; and the
line between heroic celebration and the nightmarish responsibility of heroism becomes hopelessly blurred.

Hail the Conquering Hero: Woodrow's homecoming. Libby
(Ella Raines) and Woodrow (Eddie Bracken) in the center.
(The Museum of Modern Art/Film Stills Archive)

Sturges shows us a courage in Woodrow that is provoked out of desperation. In Conquering Hero, it is less a
matter of Woodrow's meeting his heroic end than of Sturges'
gradual cornering of him, or making it impossible for him
not to confess his hoax and still remain a sympathetic character. Woodrow's confession, inevitable as it may be, primarily results from his choking constriction by everyone
around him. There is no way possible for Woodrow to live
his lie on his own terms. Bulldozed at every turn, physically and verbally, the extent to which he can exercise free
choice depends upon whether or not others will let him,
whether they will allow him to get a word in edgeways and
not constantly assault him with physical adulation. Sturges'
long tracking shots have never captured greater mass density
and awesome confusion than in the sequence when everyone in
town comes to the train depot to welcome Woodrow home.
From that moment on, his future is in their hands, as fraud
is mistaken for magnanimity. This bravery and virtue mirrored in Woodrow qualify him for public office. They mean

more than any political experience because, as Doc Bissell, the town veterinarian, remarks, "If all good men wore medals, it wouldn't be so hard to tell the good from the bad." And Woodrow's resistance to their heroic destiny only increases his appeal. Now he becomes a modest and self-effacing hero who has, in the words of one of the councilmen, "a natural flair for politics."

In the last analysis, Hail the Conquering Hero emerges as an unresolvable narrative exercise that prods at certain ideas--ideas seasoned with a particularly American flavor-- which for Sturges reveal the dilemma of our culture: the phenomenal capacity we have for excitement or, at least, for becoming excited, and how the by-products of our excitations are confusion, misapprobation, heroic celebration, excessive patriotism, and mother love. Sturges cannot judge these qualities too harshly, simply because he knows them so well. The knowledge, borne as much out of sympathy as distanced observation, brings him back and forth from the artist-commentator to the artist-swept-up-in-one-of-his-crowds. This dual function sustains a tension in Conquering Hero that allows us to experience the exhilaration of watching a brilliantly designed Preston Sturges story while seeing that in the midst of our narrative entertainment and the film's basic thematic preoccupation are greater emotional and philosophical tensions that layer and complicate the saga of Woodrow Truesmith.

Hail the Conquering Hero is, in this sense, an illustration of Perkins' attempt at defining complexity. The closing scene at the railroad station best expresses this, with a resonance that remains long after the story finishes. Unlike the earlier homecoming sequence, this farewell becomes thinned of townfolk as Woodrow, in close shot, gives his poignant salute while tenderly uttering "Semper Fidelis" to his departing marine pals. The Marine Hymn blares away too resoundingly and the marines appear too respectful for us to accept these closing shots too solemnly. Yet, in terms of the ambivalent attitude toward the film's thematic concerns, it behooves us not to ignore an element of sentimental absorption in this ending, for it seems to sum up the juggling between satire and earnestness, irony and sincerity, and even admiration and derogation--all the complexities spun into Sturges' story.

"The Great Moment"

The great moment in the story does not come with
William T. G. Morton's discovery of the anesthetic power of
ethyl chloride, but in his and all other discoverers' sacrifice
and resignation to obscurity. Here is Sturges' vindication
and honoring of this class of people with whom he sympathizes
too well. Morton's "great moment" is his sacrifice in the
name of humanity: he will lose his patent, fame and fortune,
but surgery "won't hurt a bit ... NOW ... OR EVER AGAIN!"
The Great Moment must be respected as a work that tries to
infuse melodrama with farce in a serious manner; and its
problems stem precisely from the integrity with which Sturges
attempts to develop ideas visualized as comic with a subject
poignantly felt, and from the execution of a snythesis that
finally meets with limited success.

Sturges begins the film with the story's end as he did
in The Great McGinty and in his screenplay for The Power
and the Glory. But the reversal here is more of a scram-
bling of the storytelling order, with the complications behind
the confused issue of Morton's discovery and patent never
clearly presented. The technique fails to fortify Sturges'
feeling that such people are never paid their full due by society. He shows Morton as a man of commitment and much
patience. In fact, the idea of patience--more of perseverance--
love, and gratitude infects much of the story. The first
quarter of The Great Moment exults in such sentimentality
and before long the film gels in his mold. The flashback
technique, again suggesting McGinty and The Power and the
Glory, patches unrelated scenes between the present (long
after Morton's death), the past (the time after Morton's sacrifice), and the earlier past (Morton's life before his discovery). This narrative structure distorts linearity, but
offers no decipherable key to understanding Morton's life
and struggles.

The Great Moment suffered from studio intervention--
the film was re-edited, much to Sturges' disapproval--because
it was thought to lack coherence. (Ironically, the story is
more skewed and confused in its development than originally
visualized before the studio changes.) In any case, the result
certainly diminishes our expectation for comedy in this biography. Thus, when Sturges has McCrea stumble and fall
again and again during his experiments with different chloride
gases, and William Demarest, as Eben Frost, blusters

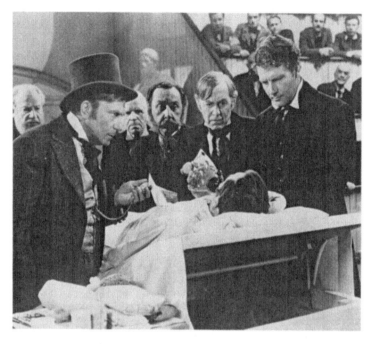

The Great Moment: discoverer for humanity. William Demarest (wearing hat), Harry Carey (center) and Joel McCrea (right). (The Museum of Modern Art/Film Stills Archive)

through the story endlessly recalling, "It was the night of September 30th, I was in excruciating pain ...," he undermines the nobility of his hero's character while satisfying his desire to inject slapstick into several sequences in the film. Consequently, McCrea's Morton becomes a serious-minded clod, not unlike Sullivan in Sullivan's Travels, but without Sullivan's comic justification. Sullivan must be naive in order to grow through his experiences; he appears foolish yet not unsympathetic in his righteous, albeit misguided aspiration to make socially-conscious pictures. Morton, however, has no reason to display his cloddishness, and there is no evidence to suggest that the real Morton was as awkward. [5] The unsynchronous tracks of serious, high-minded characterization and persistent slapstick further distort the film's tone, as Sturges' tribute to the nobility behind the perseverance and selflessness of scientists and inventors

like Morton turns into an eccentric amusement. Indeed, the
physical gags assault Morton's demeanor no less than they
suggest a certain dementedness in his personality.

The matter of tone is essential to this synthesis between melodrama and farce, and it is precisely the antip-
athy of one genre for the other in The Great Moment that
undermines the power of both and gives a puzzling tone and
bizarre quality to the story. Sturges' attempt to expand his
inventiveness, to challenge himself with ideas of comic fit-
ness and situations with comic possibilities, fails--but fails
because of the gradual change which was beginning to affect
his style at the time. (Sturges wrote the film in 1942, although it was finally finished and released in 1944.) Despite
studio intervention, The Great Moment reveals most strikingly
for the first time the restlessness that was causing Sturges
to experiment with new ways to structure his stories and to
express his comedy.

Harold Diddlebock and Ideas

Note: The Sin of Harold Diddlebock was withdrawn
for re-editing by its co-producer, Howard Hughes. The re-
vised version was released in 1950 as Mad Wednesday. References here are to the original version. Details are in the
biographical sketch.

Harold Lloyd, the personification of the American success ethic as a silent comic, finally displays his indomitable
drive in the greatest and most perplexing of fashions in The
Sin of Harold Diddlebock. In his silent films, Lloyd over-
came any obstacle to the inevitable aggressiveness of this
drive for success. Just as Chaplin was the beleaguered
tramp pathetically trying to fill the space of his shabby
clothes, to conform, to be liked; just as Keaton perceived
the cruel machinery of the world, forever defeating it, although rather bewildered, with his own physical agility; so
Lloyd triumphed in the Horatio Alger myth, through the vig-
or to succeed and the affirmation of energy to realize one's
endeavors, successful endeavors.

There is an edge of desperation to Harold Lloyd/
Diddlebock. Resurrected for this film after an eight-year
retirement, Lloyd has a field day in Harold Diddlebock, displaying a narcissism that provokes accusations of self-homage.

Sturges is respectful of this, giving him long proclamatory scenes that allow the phonic irritation of his orating to dominate over and over again. Given Sturges' oeuvre, we understand why he would be attracted to this energetic figure; however, his treatment of Lloyd comes off as a tribute to the comedian while exposing him in a rueful paradox of values. The interesting idea here lies in Lloyd's fury to display once again, over twenty years later (after such classics as Safety Last [1923], The Freshman [1925], and Speedy [1928]--all referred to in this film), this vigor idealized in still-persistent affirmation of that success drive.6 How greater can this reenactment be than by having Wally Westmore attempt to recapture through his makeup artistry the Lloyd of twenty years past? That Lloyd would want this suggests a certain grotesque egotism (not unlike that of Gloria Swanson as Norma Desmond in Billy Wilder's Sunset Boulevard); that Sturges would allow it suggests the ambivalent function of Harold Lloyd/Diddlebock in the film.

While Harold gradually desponds during his twenty-two years of stagnation in a dull accounting job, we hear "America the Beautiful" playing as the years pass by in newspaper headlines of successive presidential administrations. At present, Harold is indeed the "bottleneck" his boss has labeled him, and Sturges presents us with the irony of ambition. America, the land that nourishes this desire, structures it as an obstacle course designed to deplete the very imaginative energy that is a prerequisite for success. The paradox runs throughout Sturges' "success" stories from The Great McGinty and Christmas in July through The Great Moment to Harold Diddlebock, and it implies a value struggle of much ambivalence. At its bleakest (McGinty), the struggle shows a hopelessness about the expense of effort. Hence Harold goes from an all-American to a bottleneck. At its craziest, it suggests the possibility of a preposterousness in the expression of this all-creative energy, or perhaps more precisely, of a preposterousness enacted out of the frustration of such energy. Hence, Harold buys the perfect symbol of defiance and reassertion of ambition: a circus. Whether he remembers buying it or not matters little. His circus and Wall Street, in fact, will complement each other in a vision of harmony between wackiness and fun on the one hand and stocks and capital on the other. Harold has a thoroughly preposterous idea, but its logic is tailored to his imagination, and it works.

"There's nothing in this world as good as a strong

The Sin of Harold Diddlebock: a circus-world depiction of
Wall Street gone wild.   Jimmy Conlin; Jackie, the lion; and
Harold Lloyd.

idea," proclaims Harold, shortly after landing in jail.   Thus
Harold Lloyd/Diddlebock emerges as a comic fool of serious
intention, with Wormy as his sidekick.   Manny Farber and
W. S. Poster described Jimmy Conlin's performance in their
essay on Sturges as "that of a dessicated 200-year-old lo-
cust weighed down by an enormous copper hat. "[7]   It is the
perfect description.   Conlin has a compelling affinity for the
screen, as we watch his wrecked body recompose only to
fall apart again, in contrast with such other Sturges side-
kicks as William Demarest and Al Bridge, protrusive figures
whose eccentricities are always wedging into the story.   Wormy doesn't protrude, he simply spills all over the place trying to follow along, uncertain whether he has finally made
sense of utter confusion.

In The Sin of Harold Diddlebock, Sturges has taken
the aggressiveness represented in the antics of his hero
Lloyd, placed them in an essentially circus-world depiction

of Wall Street gone wild, and made the whole thing pay off.
"I'm for ideas ... almost bursting with them!" exclaims
Harold early in the story. At the heart of Harold Diddlebock, Sturges' own exercise in working out an idea for the
screen, lies the idea of ideas, of our need for them, and
of the driving human spirit that not only puts them into effect but insists at all costs that they work.

Sir Alfred, the Artist as a Man of Action

        At the beginning of the story, a long tracking shot
scans an orchestra pit with musicians rehearsing Tchaikovsky's Francesca da Rimini. The camera takes in every
section and almost every musician in it. We are presented
with a basic motif of the film: artists practicing their art
in craft. Unfaithfully Yours, with several such relaxed camera movements, has established the setting where its matrix
lies; it has suggested that music and performance will be the
catalysts in creating its style and theme. The sequence cul-
minates with the majestically framed Sir Alfred De Carter in
close shot, his very image dominating all, conducting. The
plot of Unfaithfully Yours concerns fidelity and obsessiveness
in love and marriage, but Sturges' film is about much more.
Later in the film when the camera closes in on Sir Alfred's
eye (the mind's eye, in every sense), we see that the story
is less concerned with the machinations of love, jealousy,
and doubt in marriage than with the artist's ability to exercise his imagination in contrivance and arrogance and to re-
prove in rage and through ill-conception--all in parody of the
special gifts that define his temperament.

        Unfaithfully Yours is simply one of the most ambitious
and sophisticated comedies ever made by an American filmmaker. Sturges took the theme of the vision and audacious-
ness of the artist and displayed through Rex Harrison's remarkable performance as Sir Alfred De Carter (inspired by
the laxative heir Sir Thomas Beecham) the sharp separation
between fantasy and actuality. As a work that distinguishes
the actions in dream life from the bunglings in real life,
Unfaithfully Yours reveals yet another kind of sophistication
in Preston Sturges' filmmaking: Sturges has made a movie
of problematic nature where he is more conscious perhaps
than at any point in his film career of the extent to which
cinematic technique can chart the terrain of the comic imagination. Unfaithfully Yours, a cruel black comedy, attempts

to integrate strategies that raise questions about their appropriateness in application to certain conceptions of comic situations.

Sturges structured Unfaithfully Yours as a comedy in three movements, three fantasies of how Sir Alfred can dispose of his presumed unfaithful wife. Each movement is filmed according to a composition that best serves the spirit of that particular fantasy. Rossini's Semiramide underscores the jealous rage of Sir Alfred as he contrives a complicated plan to kill his wife and implicate her presumed lover for the crime. "The Pilgrims' Chorus" from Wagner's Tannhäuser parodies Sir Alfred's ludicrous martyrdom as he tries to pay his wife to leave their loveless marriage with her lover. And the third fantasy is orchestrated to Tchaikovsky's Francesca da Rimini, provoking the tempest of Dante's Francesca and Paolo, and brings out the arrogance of Sir Alfred's gesture to play Russian roulette as a punishment to his adulterous wife.

These three fantasies show the ingenious and mercurial imagination of Sir Alfred, the artist and focus of the entire story. No other Sturges film is exclusively devoted to recording the performance of one actor--indeed, to shaping the story around the personality of one character. The very theme of the egocentricity of the artist depends upon this focus, and Rex Harrison executes his performance with a devastating slapstick in the last part of the film that undermines much of the verbal comedy of the first half. His performance as Sir Alfred reveals, above all, that Harrison is much more than an actor who works from the neck up. He moves throughout the first half of the film in a fluid, graceful form, and Sturges provides him with extraordinarily eloquent repartee, dialogue and speechmaking that suggest a cross between Shaw and Noel Coward: dry and playful, complexly implicit, and calling for a smooth and deft delivery. This is screenwriting of another sophistication from that of Sturges' previous films, a screenwriting that clearly establishes Sir Alfred as a verbal caretaker of the finest kind.

The critical issue with Unfaithfully Yours arises precisely from this kind of writing and the physical comedy that Sturges attempts to integrate into his creation of Sir Alfred. As a comedy of manners, Unfaithfully Yours operates at a remarkably high standard of verbal and sexual sophistication, much like The Lady Eve and The Palm Beach Story. Sturges' delightful wickedness toward Rudy Vallee, in a holdover

Unfaithfully Yours: Rex Harrison as Sir Alfred De Carter--
sublime egotism.

performance from The Palm Beach Story, matches his most
unkind treatment of Linda Darnell, who, as Lady De Carter,
is made to sound unctuously sincere in her devotion to Sir
Alfred.   (As her sister Barbara comments, "If she wasn't
my own sister, I'd have a name for her that'd make ... ")
But as slapstick farce, Unfaithfully Yours sets aside its
verbal sophistication for a chance at custard-pie comedy (when
Rex Harrison and Lionel Stander extinguish the fire in Sir Alfred's dressing room) and, more important, to show Sir Alfred, the artist, as a man of action.   Sir Alfred, who has
fantasized three ways to get rid of his wife, will now put one,
two, or all three of them into effect.   Sturges' conception is
a clever one; but Unfaithfully Yours has been functioning as
a lithe comedie noire up to now, and his intention to show the
difference between Sir Alfred's meticulous fantasies of murder
and his actual disarranged and clumsy execution of a murder
plot betrays the consistency necessary in Sir Alfred's personality and renders an implausibility to his character.   He
is too refined, too controlled even at his most passionate,

to bungle a murder plot and demolish a living room in the
process. Instead of Sir Alfred's volatile temperament in
action, we see the bipartite character Sturges is giving his
film, his compulsion perhaps to give us a healthy dose of
pratfalls.

Unlike Henry Fonda's Charley Pike in The Lady Eve,
or Eddie Bracken's roles for Sturges, Harrison as Sir Alfred
is hardly naive, incoherent, or uncoordinated, and the problem arises from attempting to fuse slapstick that suggests un-
controllability with a character who has already displayed an
intelligence based on control. (After all, the reason Sir Alfred fantasizes in the first place is out of self-restraint.)
The tempestuousness in dream life, or in a life of intrigue
and deceit, finds its greatest challenge in the act of simply
getting along at other times, in just functioning. Charley
Pike, Norval Jones, and Woodrow Truesmith find it impossible to do even that. And this is the fusion of slapstick
and character that Sturges calculated to perfection in depicting
his conception of man functioning in a paradoxical universe, and
that fails to occur in a comparable way in Unfaithfully Yours.
Sir Alfred, it would appear, is best left absorbed in the
world of his music and his dreams.

"The Beautiful Blonde from Bashful Bend"

It is a mistake to see The Beautiful Blonde from Bashful Bend as the precipitous decline of Sturges' comic talent--
or, indeed, as the demise of Preston Sturges as an important
director. Beautiful Blonde is part of a decline that started
a few years earlier in Sturges' career and had its impetus in
an unfortunate career move that found him, in 1947, at
Twentieth Century-Fox in the position of having to prove once
again his genius and box-office appeal. Sturges was unwisely
assigned a property in the rather suspect subgenre of the
western comedy to stage, along with Unfaithfully Yours, his
comeback. Handicapped by the lead, Betty Grable, the reign-
ing Fox pin-up star and herself in the decline of her career,
the problems in Beautiful Blonde owe as much to Sturges'
conception of the story and to his script as they do to the
deficiencies of his performers.

The temptation here is to criticize The Beautiful
Blonde from Bashful Bend for what it is not as much as
for what Sturges attempted and failed to pull off. To

appreciate the value of this approach, one must keep in mind
Sturges' total career to this point.   Sturges never just told a
story; his work was infused with a point of view, which, at
its most complex, was characteristically in a state of flux.
The stories of his Paramount period were indeed accomplished
products in themselves, but they were also sections of a vision of America and a display of the pliability of traditional
comic conventions in a very modern fashion.   They are works
of art because of these virtues and because of the subtle,
smooth structures--the stories--they finally are.   Even problematical works like The Great Moment and, later at Fox,
Unfaithfully Yours reveal the challenge of new ideas for screen
comedy and new techniques used.   And if they do not wholly
work, they are at least ingenious exercises of Sturges' imagination.

      The lack of imagination is the most serious mark
against Beautiful Blonde.   We see signs that come unmis-
takably as Sturges inventions: Olga San Juan's Conchita has
the best wisecracking dialogue and most of the scant wit in
the story.   Her part is very much like Diana Lynn's in Morgan's Creek and spoofs the stereotyped Latin with a sharpness
similar to Lynn's in her portrayal of a sarcastic, sophisticated
adolescent (although her portrayal of an American Indian reflects an insulting treatment of minorities still prevalent,
especially in comedies, in the postwar Hollywood of 1948).
And although Betty Grable's Freddie cannot be similarly compared to Betty Hutton's Trudy, Grable fares much better in
the role than she might be expected to.   This surely is due
to Sturges' screenwriting, for Grable has her best moment
in the film when she delivers her long plea to Judge O'Toole
(Porter Hall) against her prosecution after the first time she
shoots him.   However, much else in Beautiful Blonde that
bears Sturges' trademark does not come as an interesting
variation or extension of what we have seen before.   The
sight gags are obtrusive and the howling from the Basserman
brothers, who appear perverse in their idiocy, is strident and
pointless.   Sturges' players--Al Bridge, Porter Hall, Georgia
Caine, Torben Meyer, Dewey Robinson, etc.--look recycled
for the project.   And Rudy Vallee, even when he sings,
ceases to be an amusing target of his own tiresome image.
The result is a pale memory of familiar faces and moments
from other Sturges films.

      Sturges' stock company fails as a harmonious and dom-
inant unit to elevate the story because Beautiful Blonde is so
deeply anchored in a subgenre rarely capable of intelligent

The Beautiful Blonde from Bashful Bend: Olga San Juan, Betty Grable (with gun) and Cesar Romero. Uninspired gun-shooting.

self-parody or of using allegory, and one that is always glaringly stupid when its laughs fail. Sturges' style could not conquer such eminent liabilities or even attempt to mold the story into a unique expression of the western comedy the way he did with the melodrama in The Great Moment.

The lack of imaginative spirit in Beautiful Blonde accompanies a nonexistent point of view. Sturges did not posture his story with an attitude and it lacks tone. As satire, Beautiful Blonde is anemic; as an expansion of the western comedy, trivial; and as a depiction of frontier America, hapless and unconvincing. (An example of a film that is all three, as well as one of the finest western comedies ever made, is Douglas Sirk's Take Me to Town [1953], with Sterling Hayden and Ann Sheridan.) The film lays heavy with a plot uninspired by curious possibilities in any direction; Sturges crafted a dead-end story of few complications that matter much or give his narrative resonance.

Consequently, the tone, to the extent that one finally emerges, comes as a revenge on the project. This hostility is expressed at the onset of the movie when little Freddie's grandfather instructs her in the ways of domestic womanhood by having her perfect her shotgun technique, before, that is, she says her bedtime prayers.

The indications of Sturges' straying, and faltering, genius came with The Great Moment, but it is nonetheless unfair to chart an ascendancy and subsequent decline in his career. The Sin of Harold Diddlebock and Unfaithfully Yours reveal the vitality of a filmmaker unafraid of extending his style in new directions. Criticism of Sturges' work after Hail the Conquering Hero cannot ignore the ambitiousness of these projects. How regrettable that an apparent surrender to dullness and insipidity finally characterizes the project of The Beautiful Blonde from Bashful Bend. Here perhaps lies the moot issue of Sturges' fatigue, a drain brought on as much by his efforts to grow as a filmmaker as by the commercial forces, once under his rule, that were now to be the controlling agent of his subsequent frustrated movie career.

"The Notebooks of Major Thompson"

Pierre Daninos' observations of the Englishman's response to the French were published on the continent in the mid-1950s as a delightful series of commentary that simultaneously poked fun at each country's conception of the other. Major Marmaduke Thompson, once in service for the colonial army in India, now engages in noting the foibles and peculiarities of the French, most convincingly illustrated in the behavior of his dear friend, Monsieur Taupin (Noël-Noël). Major Thompson, of course, also emerges as his own best contradiction of the reasonableness of being English. The subject matter suggests a wealth of possibilities for complex comic screenwriting. The voice-over narration alone of Major Thompson provides challenges in visual and verbal literalness unused by Sturges since Jean's remarkable monologue as she observes Charley through her compact mirror in The Lady Eve, fourteen years earlier.

The subsequent disappointment at this unmined lode cannot be completely lessened; it can be explained only to the extent that we are sensitive to a comedy artist who,

The Notebooks of Major Thompson. Monsieur Taupin (Noël-Noël) instructs Major Thompson (Jack Buchanan) in the ways of the French.

through almost six years of frustrated professional productivity, finally came into the position of having a project financed that brought him limited enthusiasm.

Major Thompson is comparatively unfunny--funniness amounting to one of the most memorable experiences of watching any Sturges-directed movie, including those that inveigh against comfortable laughter (The Great McGinty, The Great Moment, and parts of Sullivan's Travels) in favor of a burgeoning seriousness, terribly implicit more often than not with a darker and not altogether redemptive humor. This deficiency arises from a serious lack of tension in Sturges' last film. The critical difference between laughing at the behavior of the characters in Morgan's Creek and Hail the Conquering Hero and the humor here lies in that nervous, compulsive tremor, that mood which anticipates all chaos in the world and brings out the worst and best in any people. Sturges' aloofness in Major Thompson, in both narration and dialogue, is a cool civility rather than a true

detachment. And for a Sturges movie of any kind, it's not
enough.

Observation in Morgan's Creek and Hail the Conquering Hero is a kind of commitment, one that ultimately
beckons Sturges to take a stand in his project of observing
by rendering a deeply felt perspective of individuals and society. The Notebooks of Major Thompson lacks precisely
this substance. Its sketchiness, Martine Carol's embarrassing display of temper--what must appear to be the typical French behavior here, and which is a rude joke, particularly against French women--and Jack Buchanan's leaden
major deny the comedy return of Preston Sturges its true
character and complexity. Satire fails here because it isn't
felt, and the relationship between the artist and his subject
cannot immolate the false gesture of attending to satire.
This kind of politness is, finally and regrettably, Sturges'
alone.

The lack of feeling in Major Thompson, its lack of
comic tension, negates Sturges' position as critic-director.
The continental side of Preston Sturges, present even in
his most American films, is a sensibility vying for equal
time with his brash American side on the stage of dramatic
form. Here, the entire project is as quaint and alien to its
director as the French are to Major Thompson. Buchanan's
major goes through his episodes and our curiosity about
Sturges' intention for him is never answered. Why must this
poseur invoke our comic involvement in a story that is little
more than a bogus satire, that cares too little about Major
Thompson's ideas or ours? The question is unanswered from
the point of view of any kind of Sturgesian sensibility. One
may describe how this sensibility appears when it is present,
but one cannot account for its absence.

With Sir Alfred De Carter, William Morton, or Woodrow Truesmith--all Sturges characters whose aim is to inform us in some fashion: by enacting a fantasy, by inventing,
or simply by telling the truth--Sturges grapples with the problems of order, both comic and cosmic in complexity, and
strews his comedy wreckage along the sidelines. In their
worlds, this wreckage becomes the substance and character
of Sturges the artist. The unfortunate account here, in Sturges' last film, is a gratuitousness of dialogue and action that
is sadly spiritless.

NOTES AND REFERENCES

Preface

1. Eric Jonsson (pseudonym for Andrew Sarris), "Preston Sturges and the Theory of Decline," Film Culture, No. 26 (1962), p. 19.

1

1. Mary Morris, "The Secret of Preston Sturges," PM, Sunday Picture News, 30 Dec. 1945, p. 14, col. 3.

2. Preston Sturges, Private papers. Courtesy of Mrs. Preston (Sandy) Sturges.

3-4. Preston Sturges, Private papers.

5. Mary Desti, The Untold Story: The Life of Isadora Duncan, 1921-27 (New York: Liveright, 1929), p. 22.

6-7. Preston Sturges, Private papers.

8. Preston Sturges, Private papers. His mother's book is her memoir of the last years of Isadora Duncan, The Untold Story: The Life of Isadora Duncan, 1921-27, cited above.

9. Desti, Untold Story, p. 30.

10. Desti, Untold Story, p. 32.

11. Desti, Untold Story, p. 31.

12. Desti, Untold Story, p. 47.

13-25. Preston Sturges, Private papers.

133

26. Preston Sturges, Private papers. This is, of course, the reference in the opening sequence of The Lady Eve.

27-32. Preston Sturges, Private papers.

33. Alexander King, "Preston Sturges," Vogue, 15 Aug. 1944, p. 177.

34-39. Preston Sturges, Private papers.

40. Preston Sturges, Letter to Mary Desti, 1927, Box 85, Folder 8. This and all other boxes and folders cited are in the Preston Sturges Collection of the Special Collections Library, University Research Library, University of California, Los Angeles.

41. King, p. 177.

42. Paris Singer, Letter to Preston Sturges, 5 July 1927, Box 82, Folder 30.

43. Mary Desti, Letter to Preston Sturges, 31 Oct. 1927, Box 66, Folder 30.

44. Irvin S. Cobb, Letter to Preston Sturges, 23 Feb. 1928, Box 65, Folder 1.

45. Desti, Untold Story, xiv.

46. Desti, Untold Story, xii.

47. Preston Sturges, Letter to Solomon Sturges, 1 Feb. 1930, Box 85, Folder 12.

48. Preston Sturges, Private papers.

49. Chris Chase, "The Year a Star Wasn't Born," New York Times, Sun. Ed., 5 May 1974, Sec. D, p. 11, col. 1.

50. Preston Sturges, Letter to Solomon Sturges, 18 March 1930, Box 85, Folder 12.

51. King, p. 178.

52. Carl Laemmle, Letter to Preston Sturges, 7 Dec. 1931, Box 87, Folder 13.

53. King, p. 178.

54. Preston Sturges, Letter to the Editor, Hollywood Reporter, 2 March 1933, Box 26, Folder 13.

55. W. S. Van Schmus, Telegram to Carl Laemmle, 30 Jan. 1935, Box 27, Folder 2.

56. Carl Laemmle, Memo to Preston Sturges, 14 July 1937, Box 36, Folder 13.

57. Noel F. Busch, "Preston Sturges," Life, 7 Jan. 1946, p. 92.

58. Preston Sturges, Private papers.

59. Preston Sturges, Letter to J. P. McGowen, 30 Aug. 1940, Box 100, Folder 13.

60. Preston Sturges, Private papers.

61. Box 34, Folder 2.

62. Busch, p. 92.

63. John Huston, Telegraph to Preston Sturges, 26 March 1941, Box 10, Folder 1.

64. Preston Sturges, Letter to Albert Deane, 2 March 1941, Box 39, Folder 2.

65. Preston Sturges, Sullivan's Travels, TS, Theatre Arts Library, Univ. of California, Los Angeles.

66. "Sullivan's Travels," Life, 26 Jan. 1942, p. 51.

67. Box 23, Folder 1.

68. Hermine Isaacs, review of Hail the Conquering Hero, by Preston Sturges, Theatre Arts, 28 (1944), 595-96.

69. Dudley Nichols, Letter to Preston Sturges, 29 Sept. 1944, Box 38, Folder 23.

70. Frank Lloyd Wright, Letter to Preston Sturges, 30 May 1945, Box 89, Folder 8.

71. René Fülöp-Miller (1891-1963) was a Rumanian

biographer and author on contemporary politics and
modern theatre. Fülöp-Miller coedited a translation
of the diaries of Dostoevski's wife; edited a volume
of hitherto unpublished literary fragments, letters,
and reminiscences by Tolstoy; wrote a history of the
Russian theatre with special attention to the revolu-
tionary period; and, like Mary Desti, authored a
memoir of Isadora Duncan. Triumph over Pain was
the first volume of a trilogy intended to deal with the
problems of pain, insanity, and death.

72. James Bishop, Letter to Preston Sturges, 6 Dec. 1943,
Box 37, Folder 48.

73. Preston Sturges, Unsent handwritten note, 12 Feb. 1944,
Box 31, Folder 1.

74. Morris, p. 13, col. 3.

75. Carolyn Stull, "Sturges--Genius Among Geniuses," San
Francisco Chronicle, Sun. Ed. , 23 May 1948, This
World, p. 14, cols. 3-5.

76. Morris, p. 13, col. 4.

77. Preston Sturges, Unsent handwritten note, 25 April
1944, Box 31, Folder 1.

78. Preston Sturges, Letter to Howard Hughes, 9 May 1944,
Box 72, Folder 36.

79. William Du Bois, New York Times, Sun. Ed. , 17
March 1946, Sec. 2, p. 3, col. 2.

80. Louise Graf, Letter to Preston Sturges, 22 Sept.
1945, Box 42, Folder 6.

81. Vely Bey Denizli, Letter to Preston Sturges, 4 Oct.
1946, Box 66, Folder 16.

82. Darryl F. Zanuck, Memo to Preston Sturges, 9 Nov.
1947, Box 24, Folder 3.

83. Rex Harrison, Memo to Darryl F. Zanuck, 26 Jan.
1948, Box 24, Folder 3.

84. Stull, p. 17, col. 1.

85. Seymour Stern, "Maestro's Return," New York Times, Sun. Ed., 11 July 1948, Sec. 2, p. 3, col. 1.

86. Darryl F. Zanuck, Memo to Spyros Skouras, 26 Oct. 1948, Box 1, Folder 2.

87. Earl Felton, Letter to Preston Sturges, Box 1, Folder 2.

88. Preston Sturges, Memo to Darryl F. Zanuck, 25 Aug. 1947, Box 1, Folder 2.

89. Arthur Knight, "L'Enfant de Parody," Saturday Review, 1 June 1957, p. 23.

90. Box 40, Folder 5.

91. Preston Sturges, Letter to George Templeton, 6 April 1953, Box 30, Folder 5.

92. Penelope Houston, "Preston Sturges," Sight and Sound, 34 (1965), 131.

93. Alida L. Carey, "Then and Now," New York Times Magazine, 2 Dec. 1956, p. 94.

94. Preston Sturges, Letter to Y. F. Freeman, 6 Feb. 1957, Box 37, Folder 9.

95. Box 38, Folder 31.

96. Preston Sturges, Letter to Max Gordon, 23 Sept. 1957, Box 38, Folder 31.

97. Preston Sturges, Private papers.

98. Philip Scheuer, "Zanuck's Subject: Roots of Heaven," Los Angeles Times, Sun. Ed., 12 Oct. 1958, Part 5, p. 2, col. 3.

99. Preston Sturges, Letter to John Hertz, 14 Nov. 1951, Box 30, Folder 13.

100. Preston Sturges, Letter to Howard Hawks, 5 Sept. 1956, Box 35, Folder 11.

2

1. Box 26, Folder 6, TS, p. 18.

2. Manny Farber and W.S. Poster, "Preston Sturges: Success in the Movies," Film Culture, No. 26 (1962), p. 13.

3. Andrew Sarris, "Film," Village Voice, 18 June 1964, p. 13, col. 3.

4. Philip Scheuer, "Sturges Puts Initiative into Film-making," Los Angeles Times, Sun. Ed., 26 March 1944, Sec. 3, p. 3, col. 2.

5. Farber and Poster, p. 13.

6. Andrew Sarris, "Preston Sturges in the Thirties: Filmography," Film Comment, 6, No. 4 (1970-71), 83.

7. Ferenc Molnár, Great Love, TS, p. 4, Theatre Research Collection, New York Public Library.

8. Box 26, Folder 8, TS, p. 10.

9. Alva Johnston, "How to Become a Playwright," Saturday Evening Post, 15 March 1941, p. 11.

10. Box 8, Folder 8, TS, p. 135.

11. Preston Sturges, The Good Fairy, TS, Reel 2, pp. 10-12, Theatre Research Collection, New York Public Library.

12. Box 21, Folder 7, TS, p. G-8.

13. Box 21, Folder 7, TS, pp. B-16 - B-18.

14. Preston Sturges, The Great McGinty, TS, p. 51, Theatre Arts Library, Univ. of California, Los Angeles.

15. Sturges, The Great McGinty, p. 53.

16. Northrop Frye, Anatomy of Criticism: Four Essays (Princeton: Princeton Univ. Press, 1957), p. 163.

17. Preston Sturges, The Lady Eve, TS, pp. 10-11,

Theatre Arts Library, Univ. of California, Los Angeles.

18. Frye, Anatomy, p. 180.

19. Frye, Anatomy, p. 181.

20-21. Frye, Anatomy, p. 184.

22. Northrop Frye, A Natural Perspective: The Development of Shakespearean Comedy and Romance (New York: Harcourt, Brace & World, 1965), p. 46.

23. Frye, Natural Perspective, p. 104.

24. Frye, Natural Perspective, p. 101.

25. Preston Sturges, Sullivan's Travels, TS, pp. 14-15, Theatre Arts Library, Univ. of California, Los Angeles.

26. Sturges, Sullivan's Travels, p. 38.

27. Preston Sturges, "An Author in Spite of Himself," New York Times, Sun. Ed., 1 Feb 1942, Sec. 9, p. 5, col. 1.

3

1. Stanley Cavell, "Pursuits of Happiness: A Reading of The Lady Eve," New Literary History, 10 (1979), 587.

2. In a marvelous sequence that displays Sturges' pantomimic virtuosity, Charley undergoes his initiation into the school for hurt lovers. In their train compartment on their wedding night, "Eve" tells Charley of her former love affairs as Sturges cuts from her to Pike's increasingly dismayed look, to the train chugging faster and faster. The cutting in the sequence accelerates to a frenzied pace until Pike, unable to bear any more, finally steps off the train-- and falls in the mud. All this action is orchestrated to pieces of Von Suppé's Poet and Peasant and Wagner's Tannhäuser. It is unquestionably one of the

funniest symbolic representations of sexual inter-
course ever filmed.

3. V. F. Perkins, Film as Film (London: Penguin, 1972),
    p. 119.

4. Even William Demarest's part in The Great Moment,
    for example, seems oddly suited for him, even
    though the role becomes one of the buffoonish side-
    kick destined to take a laborious pratfall upon his
    every entrance. It is a problematical role, how-
    ever, reflecting the inherent problem of the film
    itself: its inability to reconcile completely melo-
    drama with farce.

5. Nothing in Fülöp-Miller's biography of Morton suggests
    this. (René Fülöp-Miller, Triumph over Pain, trans.
    Eden and Cedar Paul [New York: Literary Guild,
    1938].)

6. The Sin of Harold Diddlebock begins with several min-
    utes of footage from Lloyd's The Freshman.

7. Farber and Poster, p. 16.

1. <u>Books</u>

AGEE, JAMES. <u>Agee on Film</u>. Vol. 1. New York: Gros-
set & Dunlap, 1958. James Agee's critical writing on
Preston Sturges for <u>The Nation</u> expresses, passionately
and persuasively, the alternating admiration and disappointment he felt with Sturges' art, here with <u>The</u>
<u>Miracle of Morgan's Creek</u> and <u>Hail the Conquering</u>
<u>Hero</u>. Acknowledging him as the most gifted film-
maker working in America at the time, Agee criti-
cized Sturges for a deficient brilliance of style, which,
on the one hand, delighted and satisfied him, yet, in
its profuse ambitiousness (of themes, emotional intentions and resonances, and comic technique), lacked
a full commitment of conscience and a more perfect
aesthetic of comedy. All this is, as Sturges might
have thought, a hard horse capsule to swallow. But
all this, too, is the kind of reckoning Agee made with
movies and that invested most of his writing for <u>The</u>
<u>Nation</u> with a measure of insight still important forty
years later. However, Agee is dangerously speculative about Sturges' childhood and wrongly overstates
the misery little Preston may have experienced. It
is here, in Agee's capsule psychologizing of Sturges'
youth, that a more accurate knowledge is crucial.

BAZIN, ANDRE. "Preston Sturges." In <u>Le Cinéma de la</u>
<u>Cruauté</u>. Paris: Flammarion, 1975, pp. 49-65.
Bazin's short pieces on <u>Sullivan's Travels</u>, <u>The Mir-</u>
<u>acle of Morgan's Creek</u>, and <u>Hail the Conquering Hero</u>
appeared in <u>L'Ecran</u> in 1948-49, when Sturges' films
were first being seen in France. Along with a later
review of <u>Mad Wednesday</u> for another publication, they
represent <u>Sturges</u> in this anthology of writings on six
filmmakers "qui ont pour point commun d'avoir imposé

un style bien particulier et un tour d'esprit subversif."
Bazin saw Sturges' genius in the distinctively American
idiom through which he expressed a critical and ironic
disposition of American life and in the classicism of
his comedy.

DURGNAT, RAYMOND. The Crazy Mirror: Hollywood Comedy and the American Image. New York: Horizon
Press, 1969. Durgnat assembles a few briefly stated
ideas on the tone and social attitudes in Sturges' work
in the essay titled, "The New Sarcasm." They may
not lead to a greater characterization of Sturges as a
film artist of disturbing tensions, but they are valuable
observations.

FARBER, MANNY and William S. Poster. "Preston Sturges:
Success in the Movies." In Manny Farber's Negative
Space. New York: Praeger, 1971, pp. 89-104. This
collection contains the Film Culture essay (No. 26
[1962], pp. 9-16).

SARRIS, ANDREW, ed. Interviews with Film Directors. New
York: Bobbs-Merrill, 1967, pp. 511-20. Sarris' book
includes his Film Culture article (No. 26 [1962], pp.
17-20), which is also partly reprinted in The American
Cinema: Directors and Directions (New York: Dutton,
1968).

2. Periodicals

BUDD, MICHAEL. "Notes on Preston Sturges and America."
Film Society Review, Jan. 1968, pp. 22-26. Budd's
article offers an explanation of Sturges' peculiarly
American temperament, which the author recognizes
as being an increasingly provocative one--rather, an
increasingly irascible one--that made Sturges and us
aware of "tensions and guilts that were only beginning
to erode the American dream." This short piece is
an incisive description of Sturges' perception of America during the wartime 1940s.

CAVELL, STANLEY. "Pursuits of Happiness: A Reading of
The Lady Eve." New Literary History, 10 (1979),
581-601. This brilliant essay on The Lady Eve stands
as one of the best pieces ever written on an individual

comedy film and its genre. Cavell draws from a
range of cinematic and dramatic references, especially
to the conventions of Shakespeare's comedies and ro-
mances, to structure a compelling argument for The
Lady Eve as representative of a cycle of Hollywood
comedies made during the 1930s and 1940s that he
calls the comedies of remarriage.

Cavell has ingeniously explored the dilemma posed
in our sympathetic acceptance of gullible Charley Pike
by raising the issue of the Barbara Stanwyck/Jean/
Eve identity as the key. The nature of the cinematic-
versus-real identity of this star/character cushions
the ontological issue of our apprehension and identification of the cinematic, of the nature and identity
of the represented object (discussed so well in Cavell's
book, The World Viewed), and of our complicity in
establishing that identity. But the intricacy of this
assertion that serves to have us reckon with (the) film
and the world removes us from the immediate reality
of Sturges' roundelay--that definitive circle that reunites the principals. Their reunion, inevitable and
inevitably most satisfying, is not so much the product
of the many possible ways of seeing and identifying,
but of the choices--the final choice--each makes to
sustain the feeling of happiness, clearly represented
in the illusion of the other. (Hence Jean/Eve's condition to Hopsie that in order to be free of her he
must ask that of her himself.)

This renders the actions in the story pointless (as
Cavell would have us believe) only if one attempts to
find a transcendence or some sort of hitherto unknown
and unsuspected awakening in the relation of the principals to and with each other. Sturges finally never
promised this. Our principals are matched for every
reason apparent in the story--reasons which don't
much change. Their attraction, however, is part of
an ineluctable affinity each has for the other, as a
potential lover and as a star (beautifully described at
one point by Cavell). That this reading of their reunion seems naive may not be the cheat; it may be
that we (and Sturges, I believe) seem to find this
understanding of romance to be an all-too-human need,
one which finally returns us to, or places us in, the
unfortunate and eternal position of gull.

FARBER, MANNY and W.S. Poster. "Preston Sturges: Success in the Movies." Film Culture, No. 26 (1962),

pp. 9-16. (Originally published in City Lights in 1954.) Manny Farber and W.S. Poster's essay is the finest appreciation of Preston Sturges' art published. Simply, no other piece has quite captured the elusive character of the Sturges phenomenon in all its dissonant glory as this essay has. To read Farber and Poster's descriptions of Sturgesian moments, moods, and characters, and of Sturges' place in modern culture, comes startlingly close to experiencing a Sturges movie.

HOUSTON, PENELOPE. "Preston Sturges." Sight and Sound, 34 (1965), 130-134. Penelope Houston's article briefly analyzes the most interesting, characteristic, and ambivalent elements of Sturges' work and discusses his sensibility as it is felt in his depictions of characters and settings, particularly of small-town America in the 1940s. This extremely well written piece is, along with the Farber and Poster essay, one of the best commentaries on Sturges' place in film.

JONSSON, ERIC (pseudonym for Andrew Sarris). "Preston Sturges and the Theory of Decline." Film Culture, No. 26 (1962), pp. 17-20. Sarris' essay on Preston Sturges follows his reminiscences of a 1957 interview with the director and is a cogent consideration on the substance and transience of the comic experience. In 1962, Sarris redeemed Sturges in part as a brilliant talent that finally burned out, one that could best be appreciated as the product of a particular time in Hollywood history. His inducement to have us consider a "theory of decline" as perhaps the imminent consequence of the best comedy filmmakers' art slights our total response to the styles of these artists. Sarris' piece suggests the idea of a changing personal style at several points, but fails to follow through with its implication that an evolving comedy style can have serious, even disturbing, intimations. This is certainly true in the middle and late careers of the directors he mentions: Chaplin, Capra, even Lubitsch. It is equally true of the Sturges of Hail the Conquering Hero and Unfaithfully Yours. And the corresponding change of sensibility in this evolution can also prove problematic, if not disastrous. This is certainly true of the Sturges of The Great Moment and The Notebooks of Major Thompson.

KRACAUER, SIEGFRIED. "Preston Sturges or Laughter Betrayed." Films in Review, 1 (1950), 11-47. Kracauer rebukes Sturges for displaying a progressively meaningless slapstick and betraying the spirit of true satire in favor of a less estimable farce. As in his other writings, Kracauer's disaffection with what he sees as the artist's abdication of a social consciousness, mars, in this case, his perceptiveness of Sturges' work. He writes out of an ideological narrowness that has been a part of his aesthetic prescription for film art. Kracauer is correct, however, in recognizing the stylistic function of Sturges' camera when he notes: "[Sturges] adroitly mobilizes his camera ... whenever he wishes to point up some gag or create a comic situation; and on such occasions, his camera assumes an independence reminiscent of its role in mature silent films." (p. 13)

SARRIS, ANDREW. "Preston Sturges in the Thirties; Filmography." Film Comment, 6, No. 4 (1970-71), 85-88. Sarris' survey of Sturges' screenwriting career of the 1930s provides a perceptive look into the distinctive features and attitudes in Sturges' work that nurtured his ultimate rise as writer-director. Sarris also offers the most responsible speculation published at the time about Sturges' contributions to his script assignments of that period.

FILMOGRAPHY

1. Plays

THE GUINEA PIG (1929).

STRICTLY DISHONORABLE (1929).

RECAPTURE (1930).

THE WELL OF ROMANCE, operetta with music by Maurice
Jacquet (1930).

CHILD OF MANHATTAN (1931).

A CUP OF COFFEE (1931).   Early play version of Christmas
in July.

SYMPHONY STORY (1932).   Early play version of Unfaithfully Yours.

MAKE A WISH (1951).   Sturges wrote the original version of
the book for this musical adaptation of his own screenplay, The Good Fairy.

2. Screenplays

Sturges had many studio assignments during his years as a
screenwriter. The following filmography includes his credited
films and virtually all of the films on which he worked that
contain a perceptible influence of his screenwriting contribution.

THE BIG POND (Paramount, 1930)
Producer: Monta Bell

Director: Hobart Henley
Screenplay: Robert Presnell and Garrett Fort. Based on the
    play The Big Pond by George Middleton and A.E.
    Thomas.
Dialogue: PRESTON STURGES and Robert Presnell
Cinematography: George Folsey
Editor: Emma Hill
Cast: Maurice Chevalier (Pierre), Claudette Colbert (Barbara
    Billings), George Barbier (Mr. Billings), Marion Bal-
    lou (Mrs. Billings), Frank Lyon (Ronnie), Nat Pendle-
    ton (Pat O'Day), Andree Corday (Toinette), Elaine Koch
    (Jennie).
Running Time: 75 minutes
Release Date: April 13, 1930

FAST AND LOOSE (Paramount, 1930)
Director: Fred Newmeyer
Screenplay: Doris Anderson and Jack Kirkland. Based on
    the play The Best People by David Gray and Avery
    Hopwood.
Dialogue: PRESTON STURGES
Cinematography: William Steiner
Cast: Miriam Hopkins (Marion Lenox), Carole Lombard
    (Alice O'Neil), Frank Morgan (Bronson Lenox), Ilka
    Chase (Millie Montgomery), Herbert Yost (George
    Grafton), David Hucheson (Lord Rockingham).
Running Time: 68 minutes
Release Date: November 29, 1930

THE POWER AND THE GLORY (Fox, 1933)
Producer: Jesse L. Lasky
Director: William K. Howard
Screenplay: PRESTON STURGES
Cinematography: James Wong Howe
Cast: Spencer Tracy (Tom Garner), Colleen Moore (Sally),
    Ralph Morgan (Henry), Helen Vinson (Eve), Clifford
    Jones (Tom Garner, Jr.), Henry Kolker (Mr. Bor-
    den), Sara Padden (Henry's wife), Billy O'Brien (Tom
    as a boy), Cullen Johnston (Henry as a boy), J. Far-
    rel MacDonald (Mulligan).
Running Time: 76 minutes
Release Date: August 18, 1933

THIRTY-DAY PRINCESS (Paramount, 1934)
Director: Marion Gering

Screenplay: PRESTON STURGES, Sam Hellman, Edwin Justus Mayer, and Frank Partos. Based on a story by Clarence Budington Kelland.
Cinematography: Leon Shamroy
Editor: Jane Loring
Cast: Sylvia Sidney (Nancy Lane/Princess Catterina), Cary Grant (Porter Madison), Edward Arnold (Richard Gresham), Vince Barnett (the Count), Henry Stephenson (King Anatol), Edgar Norton (the Baron), Ray Walker (Kirk), Lucien Littlefield (Parker), Robert McWade (Managing Editor), George Baxter (Spottswood), Marguerite Namara (Lady-in-Waiting).
Running Time: 75 minutes
Release Date: May 12, 1934

WE LIVE AGAIN (Goldwyn, 1934)
Producer: Samuel Goldwyn
Director: Rouben Mamoulian
Screenplay: Leonard Praskins
Adapters: PRESTON STURGES and Maxwell Anderson. Based on Leo Tolstoy's Resurrection.
Cinematography: Gregg Toland
Art Director: Richard Day
Production Designer: Sergei Sudeikin
Editor: Otho Lovering
Cast: Anna Sten (Katusha Maslova), Frederic March (Prince Dimitri Nekhlyudov), Jane Baxter (Missy Kortchagin), Gwendolyn Logan (Aunt Sophie), C. Aubrey Smith (Prince Kortchagin), Ethel Griffies (Aunt Marie), Jessie Ralph (Matrona Pavlovna), Sam Jaffe (Simonson), Cecil Cunningham (Theodosia), Dale Fuller (Euphemia Botchkova), Leonid Kinsky (Simon Kartinkin), Mary Forbes (Princess Kortchagin), Jessie Arnold (Korablova).
Running Time: 84 minutes
Released by United Artists on September 24, 1934.

IMITATION OF LIFE (Universal, 1934)
Producer: Carl Laemmle, Jr.
Director: John Stahl
Screenplay: William Hurlbut. Based on the novel by Fannie Hurst.
Cinematography: Merritt Gerstad
Editor: Phil Cahn
Cast: Claudette Colbert (Beatrice Pullman), Warren William

(Stephen Archer), Ned Sparks (Elmer), Louise Beavers (Aunt Delilah), Juanita Quigley (Jessie Pullman, age 3), Marilyn Knowlden (Jessie Pullman, age 8), Rochelle Hudson (Jessie Pullman, age 18), Sebie Hendricks (Peola Johnson, age 4), Dorothy Black (Peola Johnson, age 9), Fredi Washington (Peola Johnson, age 19), Alan Hale (Martin), Clarence Hummel Wilson (Landlord), Henry Armetta (Painter), Henry Kolker (Doctor), G. P. Huntley, Jr. (James), Paul Porcasi (Cafe Manager), Paullyn Garner (Mrs. Ramsey).

Running Time: 106 minutes

The extent to which STURGES' adaptation was used is unclear; however, he was not given screen credit.

THE GOOD FAIRY (Universal, 1935)
Producer: Henry Henigson
Director: William Wyler
Screenplay: PRESTON STURGES. Based on the play by Ferenc Molnár.
Cinematography: Norbert Brodine
Editor: Daniel Mandell
Cast: Margaret Sullavan (Luisa Ginglebusher), Herbert Marshall (Dr. Max Sporum), Frank Morgan (Konrad), Reginald Owen (Detlaff), Alan Hale (Schlapkohl), Beulah Bondi (Dr. Schultz), Cesar Romero (Joe), Al Bridge (Doorman), George Davis (Chauffeur), Hugh O'Connell (Gas Collector), Eric Blore (an official), Luis Alberni (Barber), Torben Meyer (Head Waiter), Frank Morgan (Moving Man).
Running Time: 98 minutes
Release Date: February 1, 1935

DIAMOND JIM (Universal, 1935)
Producer: Edmund Grainger
Director: Edward Sutherland
Screenplay: PRESTON STURGES. Based on the biography by Parker Morell.
Adapters: Harry Clork and Doris Malloy
Cinematography: George Robinson
Cast: Edward Arnold (Diamond Jim), Jean Arthur (Jane Matthews, Emma), Binnie Barnes (Lillian Russell), Cesar Romero (Jerry Richardson), Eric Blore (Sampson Fox), Hugh O'Connell (Horsley), George Sidney (Pawnbroker), William Demarest (Harry Hill), Robert McWade (A. E. Moore), Bill Hoolahahn (John L.

Sullivan).
Running Time: 93 minutes
Release Date: August 24, 1935

THE NEXT TIME WE LOVE (Universal, 1936)
Producer: Paul Kohner
Director: Edward H. Griffith
Screenplay: Melville Baker. Based on the novel by Ursula
    Parrot.
Cinematography: Joseph Valentine
Editor: Ted Hunt
Cast: Margaret Sullavan (Cicely Tyler), James Stewart
    (Christopher Tyler), Ray Milland (Tommy Abbott),
    Grant Mitchell (Michael Jennings), Anna Demetrio
    (Madame Donato), Robert McWade (Frank Carteret),
    Ronnie Cosbey (Kit), Florence Roberts (Mrs. Tal-
    bot), Christian Rub (Otto), Charles Fallon (Professor
    Dindet).
Running Time: 87 minutes
STURGES' adaptation of the novel was used to a very minor
extent.

HOTEL HAYWIRE (Paramount, 1937)
Producer: Harold Hurley
Director: George Archinbaud
Screenplay: PRESTON STURGES
Cinematography: Henry Sharp
Editor: Arthur Schmidt
Cast: Leo Carrillo (Dr. Zodiac Z. Zippe), Lynne Overman
    (Dr. Parkhouse), Mary Carlisle (Phyllis), Benny
    Baker (Bertie Sterns), Spring Byington (Mrs. Park-
    house), George Barbier (I. Ketts), Porter Hall (Judge
    Newhall), Colette Lyons (Genevieve Sterns), John Pat-
    terson (Frank Ketts), Lucien Littlefield (Elmer),
    Chester Conklin (O'Shea).
Running Time: 66 minutes
Release Date: June 15, 1937
Enormous revisions by the studio left Sturges' work severely
mutilated. Only the physical comedy written into the last
quarter of the film reflects the distinctiveness of his style.

EASY LIVING (Paramount, 1937)
Producer: Arthur Hornblow, Jr.
Director: Mitchell Leisen

Screenplay: PRESTON STURGES. Based on the story by
 Vera Caspary.
Cinematography: Ted Tetzlaff
Art Directors: Hans Dreier and Ernst Fegte
Editor: Doane Harrison
Cast: Jean Arthur (Mary Smith), Edward Arnold (J. B. Ball),
 Ray Milland (John Ball, Jr.), Luis Alberni (Louis
 Louis), Mary Nash (Mrs. Ball), Franklin Pangborn
 (Van Buren), Barlowe Borland (Mr. Gurney), William
 Demarest (Wallace Whistling), Andrew Tombes (E. F.
 Hulgar), Esther Dale (Lillian), Harlan Briggs (Office
 Manager), William B. Davidson (Mr. Hyde), Nora
 Cecil (Miss Swerf), Robert Greig (Butler).
Running Time: 66 minutes
Release Date: July 7, 1937

PORT OF SEVEN SEAS (M-G-M, 1938)
Producer: Henry Henigson
Director: James Whale
Screenplay: PRESTON STURGES and Ernest Vajda (uncred-
 ited). Based on the Marseilles Trilogy by Marcel
 Pagnol.
Cinematography: Karl Freund
Editor: Frederick Y. Smith
Cast: Wallace Beery (Cesar), Frank Morgan (Panisse),
 Maureen O'Sullivan (Madelon), John Beal (Marius),
 Jessie Ralph (Honorine), Cora Witherspoon (Claudine),
 Etienne Girardot (Bruneau), E. Allyn Warren (Cap-
 tain Escartefigue).
Running Time: 81 minutes
Release Date: June 28, 1938

IF I WERE KING (Paramount, 1938)
Producer: Frank Lloyd
Director: Frank Lloyd
Screenplay: PRESTON STURGES. Based on the play by
 Justin Huntly McCarthy.
Cinematography: Theodor Sparkuhl
Special Cinematography: Gordon Jennings
Art Directors: Hans Dreier and John Goldman
Editor: Hugh Bennett
Cast: Ronald Colman (François Villon), Basil Rathbone
 (Louis XI), Frances Dee (Katherine), Ellen Drew
 (Huguette), C. V. France (Father Villon), Henry Wil-
 coxon (Captain of the Watch), Heather Thatcher (the

Queen), Stanley Ridges (René de Montigny), Bruce
Lester (Noel le Jolys), Walter Kingsford (Tristan
L'Hermite), Alma Lloyd (Colette), Sidney Toler (Robin
Turgis).
Running Time: 100 minutes
Release Date: September 19, 1938

NEVER SAY DIE (Paramount, 1939)
Producer: Paul Jones
Director: Elliot Nugent
Screenplay: PRESTON STURGES, Don Hartmann, and Frank
Butler
Cinematography: Leo Tover
Editor: James Smith
Cast: Martha Raye (Mickey Hawkins), Bob Hope (John Kid-
ley), Ernest Cassart (Jeepers), Paul Harvey (Jasper
Hawkins), Andy Devine (Henry Munch), Siegfried Ru-
mann (Poppa), Alan Mowbray (Prince Smirnow), Gale
Sondergaard (Juno).
Running Time: 80 minutes
Release Date: March 7, 1939

REMEMBER THE NIGHT (Paramount, 1940)
Producer: Mitchell Leisen
Director: Mitchell Leisen
Screenplay: PRESTON STURGES
Cinematography: Ted Tetzlaff
Art Directors: Hans Dreier and Roland Anderson
Music: Frederick Hollander
Editor: Doane Harrison
Cast: Barbara Stanwyck (Lee Leander), Fred MacMurray
(John Sargent), Beulah Bondi (Mrs. Sargent), Eliza-
beth Patterson (Aunt Emma), Willard Robertson (Fran-
cis X. O'Leary), Sterling Holloway (Willie), Charles
Waldron (Judge in New York), Paul Guilfoyle (District
Attorney), Charles Arnt (Tom), John Wray (Hank),
Thomas W. Ross (Mr. Emory), Snowflake (Rufus),
Tom Kennedy (Fat Mike), Georgia Caine (Lee's
mother), Virginia Brissac (Mrs. Emory), Spencer
Charters (Judge at rummage sale).
Running Time: 86 minutes
Release Date: January 9, 1940

3.   Films Written and Directed by Preston Sturges

THE GREAT McGINTY (Paramount, 1940)
Original Titles: Down Went McGinty, The Biography of a
     Bum, The Mantle of Dignity, The Story of a Man,
     The Vagrant.
Producer: Paul Jones
Assistant Director: George Templeton
Cinematography: William Mellor
Art Directors: Hans Dreier and Earl Hedrick
Costumes: Edith Head
Music: Frederick Hollander
Sound: Earl Hayman and Richard Olson
Editor: Hugh Bennett
Cast: Brian Donlevy (Dan McGinty), Muriel Angelus (Cath-
     erine McGinty), Akim Tamiroff (the Boss), William
     Demarest (the Politician), Allyn Joslyn (George),
     Louis Jean Heydt (Thompson), Harry Rosenthal (Louie,
     the bodyguard), Arthur Hoyt (Mayor Tillinghast), Lib-
     by Taylor (Bessie, the maid), Thurston Hall (Mr.
     Maxwell), Esther Howard (Madame La Jolla), Frank
     Moran (the Boss's chauffeur), Dewey Robinson (Benny
     Felgman), Richard Carle (Dr. Jarvis), Jimmy Conlin
     (the lookout), Robert Warwick (Honeywell's spokes-
     man), Donnie Kerr (Catherine's son, age 4), Mary
     Thomas (Catherine's daughter, age 6), Drew Roddy
     (Catherine's son, age 9), Sheila Sheldon (Catherine's
     daughter, age 11).
Running Time: 81 minutes
Release Date: July 23, 1940
The Great McGinty won the Academy of Motion Picture Arts
and Sciences' award for the best original screenplay of 1940.

CHRISTMAS IN JULY (Paramount, 1940)
Original Titles: A Cup of Coffee, Ants in Their Pants, The
     New Yorkers.
Producer: Paul Jones
Assistant Director: George Templeton
Cinematography: Victor Milner
Art Directors: Hans Dreier and Earl Hedrick
Music Director: Sigmund Krumgold
Sound: Harry Lindgren and Walter Oberst
Editor: Ellsworth Hoagland
Cast: Dick Powell (Jimmy MacDonald), Ellen Drew (Betty
     Casey), Raymond Walburn (Mr. Maxford), Alexander

Carr (Mr. Schindel), William Demarest (Mr. Bildocker),
Ernest Truex (Mr. Baxter), Franklin Pangborn (Radio
Announcer), Harry Hayden (Mr. Waterbury), Rod
Cameron (Dick), Michael Morris (Tom), Harry Rosen-
thal (Harry), Georgia Caine (Mrs. MacDonald), Ferike
Boros (Mrs. Schwartz), Torben Meyer (Mr. Schmidt),
Julius Tannen (Mr. Zimmerman), Al Bridge (Mr. Hill-
beiner), Lucille Ward (Mrs. Casey), Vic Potel (Furni-
ture Salesman), Sheila Sheldon (Sophie), Esther Michel-
son (Sophie's mother), Frank Moran (Officer Murphy),
George Renavent (Sign Painter). Also with Arthur
Hoyt, Robert Warwick, Jimmy Conlin, and Dewey
Robinson.
Running Time: 67 minutes
Release Date: September 20, 1940

THE LADY EVE (Paramount, 1941)
Original Title: Two Bad Hats
Producer: Paul Jones
Cinematography: Victor Milner
Art Directors: Hans Dreier and Ernst Fegte
Costumes: Edith Head
Music Director: Sigmund Krumgold
Editor: Stuart Gilmore
Cast: Barbara Stanwyck (Jean/Eve), Henry Fonda (Charles
Pike), Charles Coburn ("Colonel" Harrington), Eugene
Pallette (Mr. Pike), William Demarest (Mugsy), Eric
Blore (Sir Alfred Glennan Keith), Melville Cooper
(Gerald), Martha O'Driscoll (Martha), Janet Beecher
(Mrs. Pike), Robert Greig (Burrows), Dora Clement
(Gertrude), Luis Alberni (Mr. Pike's chef), Frank
Moran (the bartender at the party), Pauline Drake
(Social Secretary), Harry Rosenthal (Piano Tuner),
Abdullah Abbas (the man with the potted palm). With
Wilda Bennett, Georgia Cooper, Evelyn Beresford,
Gayne Whitman, Alfred Hall, Bertram Marburgh,
George Melford, Kenneth Gibson, and Arthur Stuart
Hull as the party guests; Julius Tannen, Ray Flynn,
Harry Bailey, and Arthur Hoyt as Pike's lawyers;
and Jimmy Conlin, Al Bridge, and Vic Potel as the
ship's stewards.
Running Time: 97 minutes
Release Date: February 27, 1941
The Lady Eve is based on a story by Monckton Hoffe.

SULLIVAN's TRAVELS (Paramount, 1941)
Producer: Paul Jones
Cinematography: John Seitz
Process Photography: Farciot Edouart
Art Directors: Hans Dreier and Earl Hedrick
Music: Leo Shuken and Charles Bradshaw
Music Director: Sigmund Krumgold
Editor: Stuart Gilmore
Cast: Joel McCrea (John L. Sullivan), Veronica Lake (the Girl), Robert Warwick (Mr. Lebrand), William Demarest (Mr. Jones), Franklin Pangborn (Mr. Casalsis), Porter Hall (Mr. Hadrian), Byron Foulger (Mr. Valdelle), Margaret Hayes (Secretary), Robert Greig (Sullivan's butler), Eric Blore (Sullivan's valet), Torben Meyer (the doctor), Vic Potel (the cameraman), Richard Webb (the radioman), Charles Moore (the chef), Almira Sessions (Ursula), Esther Howard (Miz Zeffie), Frank Moran (Chauffeur), George Renavent (the old tramp), Al Bridge (Chain Gang Overseer), Jimmy Conlin (Trusty), Jan Buckingham (Mrs. Sullivan), Robert Winkler (Bud), Snowflake (the porter), Harry Hayden (Mr. Carson), Willard Robertson (Judge), Arthur Hoyt (Preacher), Dewey Robinson (Sheriff).
Running Time: 91 minutes
Release Date: December 5, 1941

THE PALM BEACH STORY (Paramount, 1942)
Producer: Paul Jones
Cinematographer: Victor Milner
Art Directors: Hans Dreier and Ernst Fegte
Makeup: Wally Westmore
Music Director: Victor Young
Gowns: Irene
Sound: Harry Lindgren and Walter Oberst
Editor: Stuart Gilmore
Cast: Claudette Colbert (Geraldine Jeffers), Joel McCrea (Tom Jeffers), Mary Astor (Princess Centimillia), Rudy Vallee (J.D. Hackensacker III), Franklin Pangborn (Apartment Manager), Robert Dudley (the "Wienie King"), Sig Arno (Toto), Esther Howard (the Wienie King's wife), Monte Blue (Doorman), Harry Tyler (Ticket Agent). With William Demarest, Robert Warwick, Arthur Stuart Hull, Torben Meyer, Jimmy Conlin, Vic Potel, Jack Norton, Robert Greig, Roscoe Ates, Dewey Robinson, Chester Conklin, and Sheldon Jett

as the members of the Ale and Quail Club; and Frank
Moran, Arthur Hoyt, and Al Bridge as the train con-
ductors.
Running Time: 90 minutes
Release Date: November 2, 1942

THE MIRACLE OF MORGAN'S CREEK (Paramount, 1944)
Cinematography: John Seitz
Art Directors: Hans Dreier and Ernst Fegte
Set Designer: Stephen Seymour
Costumes: Edith Head
Makeup: Wally Westmore
Music: Leo Shuken and Charles Bradshaw
Sound: Hugo Grensback and Walter Oberst
Editor: Stuart Gilmore
Cast: Eddie Bracken (Norval Jones), Betty Hutton (Trudy
Kockenlocker), Diana Lynn (Emmy Kockenlocker),
William Demarest (Constable Kockenlocker), Porter
Hall (Justice of the Peace), Emory Parnell (Mr.
Tuerck), Julius Tannen (Mr. Rafferty), Al Bridge
(Mr. Johnson), Vic Potel (Newspaper Editor), Almira
Sessions (Wife of the Justice of the Peace), Esther
Howard (Sally), J. Farrell MacDonald (Sheriff), Frank
Moran (Military Policeman), Connie Tompkins (Cecil-
ia), Georgia Caine (Mrs. Johnson), Torben Meyer
(the doctor), Jimmy Conlin (the Mayor), Harry Rosen-
thal (Mr. Schwartz), Chester Conklin (Pete), Byron
Foulger and Arthur Hoyt (McGinty's secretaries).
With Brian Donlevy and Akim Tamiroff as Governor
McGinty and the Boss.
Running Time: 99 minutes
Release Date: January 5, 1944
The film was completed in early 1943, but faced censorship
problems that prevented its release for almost a year. The
Miracle of Morgan's Creek received an Academy Award nom-
ination for the best original screenplay of 1944.

HAIL THE CONQUERING HERO (Paramount, 1944)
Original Title: The Little Marine
Cinematography: John Seitz
Art Directors: Hans Dreier and Haldane Douglas
Set Designer: Stephen Seymour
Music: Werner Heymann
Music Director: Sigmund Krumgold
Sound: Wallace Nogle

Editor: Stuart Gilmore
Cast: Eddie Bracken (Woodrow Truesmith), Ella Raines (Lib-
by), Bill Edwards (Forrest Noble), Raymond Walburn
(Mayor Noble), William Demarest (Sergeant), Jimmie
Dundee (Corporal), Georgia Caine (Mrs. Truesmith),
Al Bridge (Noble's campaign manager), Freddie Steele
(Bugsy), James Damore (Jonesy), Stephen Gregory
(Bill), Len Hendry (Juke), Esther Howard (Mrs. Noble),
Elizabeth Patterson (Libby's aunt), Jimmy Conlin (Judge
Dennis), Arthur Hoyt (Reverend Upperman), Harry Hay-
den (Doc Bissell), Franklin Pangborn (Committee
Chairman), Torben Meyer (Mr. Schultz), Robert War-
wick (the officer at the train depot), Chester Conklin
(the delivery boy), Paul Porcasi (Restaurant Manager),
Dewey Robinson (Conductor), Frank Moran (the sign
painter), George Anderson (Bartender), Julie Gibson
(Lounge Singer). With Vic Potel and Jack Norton as
the band leaders; and Tom McGuire, Philo McCul-
lough, Franklyn Farnum, and Kenneth Gibson as the
town councilmen.
Running Time: **101 minutes**
Release Date: June 7, 1944
Hail the Conquering Hero received an Academy Award nom-
ination for the best original screenplay of 1944.

THE GREAT MOMENT (Paramount, 1944)
Original Title: Triumph over Pain
Cinematography: Victor Milner
Art Directors: Hans Dreier and Ernst Fegte
Set Designer: Stephen Seymour
Music: Victor Young
Sound: Harry Lindgren and Walter Oberst
Editor: Stuart Gilmore
Cast: Joel McCrea (William T. G. Morton), Betty Field
(Mrs. Morton), Harry Carey (Professor Warren),
William Demarest (Eben Frost), Louis Jean Heydt
(Horace Wells), Julius Tannen (Dr. Jackson), Ed-
win Maxwell (Vice-President of the Medical Society),
Porter Hall (President Franklin Pierce), Franklin
Pangborn (Dr. Heywood), Grady Sutton (Homer Quin-
by), Harry Hayden (Judge Shipman), Torben Meyer
(Dr. Dahlmeyer), Donivee Lee (Betty Morton), Vic
Potel (Dental Patient), Thurston Hall (Senator Bor-
land), J. Farrell MacDonald (the priest), Robert
Frandsen (Mr. Abbot), Sylvia Field (Mother of the
little girl patient), Reginald Sheffield (Father of the

little girl patient), Robert Greig (Morton's butler), Harry Rosenthal (Mr. Chamberlain), Frank Moran (the hospital porter), Dewey Robinson (Colonel Lawson), Al Bridge (Mr. Sone), Georgia Caine (Mrs. Whitman), Chester Conklin (a patient), Sheldon Jett (the patient with the swollen jaw), Esther Howard (the streetwalker), Jimmy Conlin (Mr. Burnett), Arthur Hoyt (President Pierce's secretary), Donnie Kerr (the young boy patient), Billy Sheffield (Morton's son), Janet Chapman (Morton's daughter), Tricia Moore (Morton's daughter, older).

Running Time: 83 minutes
Release Date: June 9, 1944
Although completed in June of 1942, the film was released two years later after significant reediting. Credits are listed from among those in the original version.

THE SIN OF HAROLD DIDDLEBOCK (California Pictures Corp. , 1947)
Producers: PRESTON STURGES and Howard Hughes
Production Manager: Cliff Broughton
Cinematography: Robert Pittack
Special Effects: John Fulton
Art Director: Robert Usher
Set Designer: Victor A. Gangelin
Makeup: Ted Larsen and Wally Westmore
Hair Styles: Elaine Ramsay
Music: Werner Heymann. Additional music by Harry Rosenthal.
Sound: Fred Lau
Technical Director: Curtis Courant
Editor: Thomas Neff
Cast: Harold Lloyd (Harold Diddlebock), Frances Ramsden (Miss Otis), Jimmy Conlin (Wormy), Raymond Walburn (E.J. Waggleberry), Edgar Kennedy (Bartender), Arline Judge (Manicurist), Franklin Pangborn (Formfit Franklyn), Lionel Stander (Max), Margaret Hamilton (Harold's sister), Al Bridge (Circus Manager), Frank Moran (Mike, the policeman), Torben Meyer (the barber), Vic Potel (Professor Potelle), Jack Norton (James Smoke), Arthur Hoyt (Mr. Blackston), Robert Greig (the coachman), Georgia Caine (the bearded lady), Gladys Forrest (the snake charmer). With Robert Dudley and Rudy Vallee as the bankers.
Running Time: 89 minutes
Release Date: April 4, 1947

The Sin of Harold Diddlebock was withdrawn for reediting, then rereleased through RKO-Radio in 1950 under the title Mad Wednesday, with a running time of 78 minutes.

UNFAITHFULLY YOURS (Twentieth Century-Fox, 1948)
Original Title: Symphony Story
Producer: PRESTON STURGES
Cinematography: Victor Milner
Special Effects: Fred Sersen
Art Directors: Lyle Wheeler and Joseph C. Wright
Set Designers: Thomas Little and Paul S. Fox
Costumes: Bonnie Cashin
Makeup: Ben Nye
Music Director: Alfred Newman. With music from Rossini's
    Semiramide Overture, Wagner's Tannhäuser, and
    Tchaikovsky's Francesca da Rimini.
Sound: Arthur L. Kirbach and Roger Roman
Editor: Robert Fritch
Conducting instructions for Rex Harrison provided by Robin
    Sanders Clark.
Cast: Rex Harrison (Sir Alfred De Carter), Linda Darnell
    (Daphne De Carter), Barbara Lawrence (Barbara),
    Rudy Vallee (August), Kurt Krueger (Anthony), Lionel
    Stander (Hugo), Edgar Kennedy (Sweeney), Al Bridge
    (House Detective), Julius Tannen (the tailor), Torben
    Meyer (Dr. Schultz), Robert Greig (Jules), Evelyn
    Beresford (Mme Pompadour), Georgia Caine (Dowager),
    Harry Seymour (Musician), Isabel Jewell and Marion
    Marshall (Telephone Operators).
Running Time: 105 minutes
Release Date: October 1, 1948

THE BEAUTIFUL BLONDE FROM BASHFUL BEND (Twen-
    tieth Century-Fox, 1949)
Producer: PRESTON STURGES
Cinematography: Harry Jackson
Technicolor Color Director: Natalie Kalmus
Associate Color Director: Leonard Doss
Special Effects: Fred Sersen
Art Directors: Lyle Wheeler and George W. Davis
Set Designers: Thomas Little and Stuart Reiss
Costumes: Rene Hubert
Wardrobe Director: Charles Le Maire
Makeup: Ben Nye
Music: Cyril Mockridge

Orchestral Arrangements: Herbert Spencer
Editor: Robert Fritch
Cast: Betty Grable (Freddie), Cesar Romero (Blackie), Rudy
Vallee (Charles Hingleman), Olga San Juan (Conchita),
Sterling Holloway and Danny Jackson (the Basserman
brothers), Hugh Herbert (Doctor), El Brendel (Mr.
Jorgensen), Porter Hall (Judge O'Toole), Emory Par-
nell (Mr. Hingleman), Al Bridge (Sheriff), Chris-Pin
Martin (Joe), Pati Behrs (Roulette), Margaret Hamil-
ton (Mrs. O'Toole), J. Farrell MacDonald (Sheriff
Sweetzer), Richard Hale (Mr. Basserman), Georgia
Caine (Mrs. Hingleman), Esther Howard (Mrs. Smid-
lap), Harry Hayden (Train Conductor), Chester Conk-
lin (Messenger), Torben Meyer (Dr. Schultz), Dewey
Robinson (Bartender), Richard Kean (Dr. Smidlap),
Russell Simpson (Grandpa), Mary Monica MacDonald
(Freddie as a little girl), Marie Windsor (French
Saloon Singer).
Running Time: 77 minutes
Release Date: May 31, 1949
The Beautiful Blonde from Bashful Bend is based on a story
by Earl Felton.

THE NOTEBOOKS OF MAJOR THOMPSON (LES CARNETS DU
MAJOR THOMPSON, S. N. E. Gaumont, Alain Poire-Paul
Wagner, 1957)
Producers: Alain Poire and Paul Wagner
Assistant Directors: Pierre Kast and Francis Caillaud
Cinematography: Maurice Barry and Christian Matras
Art Director: Serge Pimenoff
Music: George Van Parys
Sound: Jean Rieul
Editor: Raymond Lanny
Cast: Jack Buchanan (Major Thompson), Martine Carol
(Martine), Noël-Noël (Monsieur Taupin), Genevieve
Brunet (Mlle Sylvette), Catherine Boyl (Ursula),
Totti Truman Taylor (Miss Ffyfth), Paulette Dubost
(Madame Taupin), André Luguet (Monsieur Fusillard),
Running Time: 83 minutes
Release Date: May 21, 1957 in the United States by Con-
tinental Distributors.

4. Other Productions

I MARRIED A WITCH (Paramount, 1942)

Producer: René Clair
Director: René Clair
Screenplay: Marc Connelly, Robert Pirosh, and (uncredited)
    Dalton Trumbo. Based on a story by Thorne Smith
    and Norman Matson.
Cinematography: Ted Tetzlaff
Special Effects: Gordon Jennings
Art Directors: Hans Dreier and Ernst Fegte
Costumes: Edith Head
Editor: Eda Warren
Cast: Fredric March (Wallace Wooley), Veronica Lake (Jen-
    nifer), Robert Benchley (Dr. Dudley White), Susan
    Hayward (Estelle Masterson), Cecil Kellaway (Daniel),
    Elizabeth Patterson (Margaret), Robert Warwick (J.B.
    Masterson), Eily Malyon (Tabitha), Robert Greig (the
    town crier), Helen St. Rayner (the vocalist), Aldrich
    Bowker (the Justice of the Peace), Emma Dunn (the
    wife of the Justice of the Peace).
Running Time: 84 minutes
Released through United Artists.
STURGES was originally the producer on this project and was
involved with the writing, casting, and other responsibilities,
but other production commitments obliged him to leave it.

STAR-SPANGLED RHYTHM (Paramount, 1942)
Producer: Joseph Sistrom
Director: George Marshall
Screenplay: Harry Turgend
Cinematography: Leo Tover
Music: Robert Emmett Dolan. With songs by Johnny Mer-
    cer and Harold Arlen.
Editor: Arthur Schmidt
Cast: All-star extravaganza of players and directors from
    Paramount performing in support of the war effort.
    STURGES appears as himself.

VENDETTA (RKO-Radio, 1950)
Producer: Howard Hughes
Director: Mel Ferrer (and, uncredited, PRESTON STURGES,
    Max Ophüls, and Stuart Heisler)
Screenplay: W.R. Burnett and (uncredited) PRESTON STUR-
    GES. Based on Colomba by Prosper Mérimée.
Cinematography: Franz Planer and Al Gilks
Art Director: Robert Usher
Music: Roy Webb. Based on Puccini's operas.

Editor: Stuart Gilmore
Cast: Faith Domergue (Colomba Della Rabbia), George
      Dolenz (Orso Della Rabbia), Hillary Brooke (Lydia
      Nevil), Nigel Bruce (Sir Thomas Nevil), Donald
      Buka (Pachino), Joseph Calleia (Mayor Barracini),
      Hugo Haas (Brando), Robert Warwick (Prefect).
Running Time: 84 minutes
STURGES' involvement in the production of Vendetta is
covered in the profile.

PARIS HOLIDAY (Tolda, 1958)
Producer: Bob Hope
Director: Gerd Oswald
Screenplay: Edmund Beloin and Dean Riesner. Based on
      a story by Bob Hope.
Cinematography: Roger Hubert
Music: Joseph J. Lilley. With songs by James Van Heusen
      and Sammy Cahn.
Editor: Ellsworth Hoaglund
Cast: Bob Hope (Robert Leslie Hunter), Fernandel, Anita
      Ekberg (Zara), Martha Hyer (Ann McCall), André
      Morell (Ambassador), PRESTON STURGES (Serge
      Vitry).
Running Time: 100 minutes
Released through United Artists.

INDEX

Screen Classics

Screen Classics is a series of critical biographies, film histories, and analytical studies focusing on neglected filmmakers and important screen artists and subjects, from the era of silent cinema to the golden age of Hollywood to the international generation of today. Books in the Screen Classics series are intended for scholars and general readers alike. The contributing authors are established figures in their respective fields. This series also serves the purpose of advancing scholarship on film personalities and themes with ties to Kentucky.

Series Editor
Patrick McGilligan

Books in the Series

Mae Murray: The Girl with the Bee-Stung Lips
Michael G. Ankerich

Hedy Lamarr: The Most Beautiful Woman in Film
Ruth Barton

Von Sternberg
John Baxter

The Marxist and the Movies: A Biography of Paul Jarrico
Larry Ceplair

Warren Oates: A Wild Life
Susan Compo

Jack Nicholson: The Early Years
Robert Crane and Christopher Fryer

Being Hal Ashby: Life of a Hollywood Rebel
Nick Dawson

Intrepid Laughter: Preston Sturges and the Movies
Andrew Dickos

John Gilbert: The Last of the Silent Film Stars
Eve Golden

Mamoulian: Life on Stage and Screen
David Luhrssen

My Life as a Mankiewicz: An Insider's Journey through Hollywood
Tom Mankiewicz and Robert Crane

William Wyler: The Life and Films of
Hollywood's Most Celebrated Director
Gabriel Miller

Raoul Walsh: The True Adventures of
Hollywood's Legendary Director
Marilyn Ann Moss

Some Like It Wilder: The Life and Controversial Films
of Billy Wilder
Gene D. Phillips

Arthur Penn: American Director
Nat Segaloff

Claude Rains: An Actor's Voice
David J. Skal with Jessica Rains

Buzz: The Life and Art of Busby Berkeley
Jeffrey Spivak

Thomas Ince: Hollywood's Independent Pioneer
Brian Taves

Carl Theodor Dreyer and Ordet:
My Summer with the Danish Filmmaker
Jan Wahl

CPSIA information can be obtained at www.ICGtesting.com
Printed in the USA
BVOW000908270313

316541BV00006B/11/P

9 780813 141947